Foreword by Ronnie and Karen Lott

W9-AAO-253

unshakable

The Building Blocks of an Enduring Marriage

KEITH POTTER

credo
house publishers

Unshakable: The Building Blocks of an Enduring Marriage

Copyright © 2009 by Keith Potter

All rights reserved. No part of this book may be reproduced in any form without permission in writing from the publisher, except in the case of brief quotations embodied in critical articles or reviews.

Published by Credo House Publishers, a division of Credo Communications, LLC, Grand Rapids, Michigan; www.credocommunications.net.

ISBN-10: 1-935391-30-5
ISBN-13: 978-1-935391-30-2

Scripture is taken from the HOLY BIBLE, NEW INTERNATIONAL VERSION®. NIV®. Copyright © 1973, 1978, 1984 by International Bible Society. Used by permission of Zondervan. All rights reserved.

Cover design: Frank Gutbrod
Interior design: Frank Gutbrod
Cover photo: ©iStockphoto

Printed in the United States of America

What others are saying about *Unshakable* . . .

"This book gives concrete Christian advice and real steps to help balance a relationship. Read carefully and discussed thoroughly, the ideas in this book will help couples move forward with a new love and understanding for each other.

—**Ronnie & Karen Lott (from the Foreword)**

"Based on years of experience, Keith Potter asks and answers the hard questions about marriage relationships. He balances frank advice with heartfelt concern. The result is *Unshakable*—a book that will help every couple deepen their love and commitment to each other."

—**Alice Gray, best-selling author and co-author of**
The Walk Out Woman* and *The Worn Out Woman

"Keith Potter's experience and solid biblical advice make this book something every couple should read. The 'Stop, Talk and Listen' and 'What Ifs and What Abouts' sections are the best I've seen in thirty years for helping couples communicate through the most common relational difficulties. His humility and candor are an extra bonus."

—**Dr. Marty Trammell, English and Communication Chair,**
Corban University

"This is the best book on marriage since Charlie Shedd wrote *Letters to Karen* and *Letters to Philip*. It is a 'must read' for pastors and marriage counselors, and useful for every married couple."

—**The Rev. Neal Snider, author of**
Daily Walks with Saints and Sinners

"If you want to strengthen your marriage, *Unshakable* is a must read. Keith Potter gives the reader the collective wisdom of years of counseling. Collating years of counseling notes, he reveals the 'core values' that cut across the boundaries of race, religion and philosophy. Understanding these values will strengthen any marriage—including those facing failure."

—**Dr. Rich Rollins, pastor and co-author of**
Redeeming Relationships

"With 25 years of experience walking couples into marriage, Keith Potter's wisdom is an investment in your own marriage. Potter shines a light on the 18 core values all healthy marriages have in common."

—**D. J. Young, marriage and family author and speaker,**
Vancouver, Washington

To
Sue, my wife. You gift wrap my life.
Thank you for loving me with so much
courage, tenderness and flair.

contents

foreword

We have known Keith Potter since he came to Saratoga Federated Church many years ago. Keith has become our pastor, counselor, friend, and now marriage coach. He has been consistent in his quest for understanding relationships and has a deep desire to improve on himself in all areas of his life.

As kids we were taught the rules of how to play fair, to get along and not to fight. Most of these lessons stay with us throughout our lives, but seem to somehow change dramatically when we get married. Somehow the basic instincts to sustain, nurture, and to play fair can be thrown out the window when our spouse glances at us in the wrong way. We have learned through the building blocks discussed in this book that we have to strengthen the muscles of respect, trust, and patience, and that these help make the foundation of a marriage strong.

Keith points out that listening is critical but that men and women hear, process, and react very differently. One of our favorite illustrations Keith uses is how most men will take information in, look at it and quickly flush it. Most women will take the same information, look at it and need to watch it swirl around and around, then, when ready, flush it. This is just one of the many memorable images that Keith uses in his teaching.

We have always believed that to forgive and "move forward fast" is an important factor in our marriage, but Keith gives actual steps to facilitate forgiveness. He states that forgiveness can become a lifestyle of grace, an act of mercy, and that prayer is critical in a relationship that forgives, heals and learns. We've learned to forgive always and completely ... even when we feel it may be undeserved!

Each chapter segment ends with a "Stop, Talk and Listen" box with questions that help you and your spouse examine yourselves clearly. If answered honestly, these specific questions will bring worthwhile discussion and evoke realism and truth about you, your spouse and your marriage.

In our marriage, we now use many of the principles and tools Keith writes about. And our communication level has changed dramatically! We feel we are moving forward one step at a time and have become better able to understand each other's love languages. We also know better how to accept, compromise, negotiate, sacrifice and forgive more effectively. We are trying to focus on hope rather than the expectations with which we began our marriage. With this book we are trying to do the hard work of "mirror time" and hope to become great at the game of marriage.

Keith and Sue interact in their marriage with a skilled and learned behavior that they have obviously been practicing for years. They have taken the time to build a solid foundation that we feel is ... well, unshakeable.

This book gives concrete Christian advice and real steps to help balance a relationship. Read carefully and discussed thoroughly, the ideas in this book will help couples move forward with a new love and understanding for each other. Like Keith and Sue, we are doing this marriage on purpose!

Ronnie Lott, NFL Hall of Fame, and
Karen Lott, wife, mother and philanthropist

preface

About Core Values

At twenty-two, I prepared to perform my first wedding ceremony. Fresh out of school and newly married, with barely a whisker and a frequent crack in my voice, I wondered: *What do I have to offer this couple during premarriage counseling?*

I didn't feel particularly wise. My naïve idealism had already been tested by months of marriage. Already there had been surprises of every kind. I was a true novice.

A scan of the bookstores revealed an interesting array of marital self-help titles. But most were more therapeutic than preparatory. And many were so loaded with syrupy Christian jargon that they would be of little use to couples for whom such language is unfamiliar (even unattractive).

A seasoned pastor, Gary Wells, prepared Sue and me for marriage in ways that seemed less scripted than the programs on the shelf. He asked us questions and drew out of us as much, or more, than he passed on in his didactic lectures.

So, taking a lesson from Gary, I began my first premarriage session like this:

> "Look, I'm new at this too. Far from being an
> expert, I'm a student of marriage. So you tell me.
> What are the building blocks of a strong marriage?"

I sat with a pen and an empty yellow pad. The couple spoke and I took notes. When the list seemed to be filling in, I stopped them and took "block" number one (probably trust, almost always the first to be mentioned). I simply asked them, "What does 'trust' mean and why is it important?" Together, we three students began talking and taking mental notes as we told our stories, definitions, observations, opinions and convictions. And when "trust" had been thoroughly covered, we moved on to the next "block" (usually communication).

Four hundred weddings later, I'm asking the same questions and still taking notes. While every person and couple brings a unique vocabulary and order to their lists, fundamental patterns have developed. There are consistent observations and convictions held, to varying degrees, by virtually all couples entering into matrimony.

This book takes *their observations* public. In doing so, I've been careful not to betray particular incidents and peculiarities that ought to be held in confidence. Nonetheless, this work does radiate with currents and themes and tones of common agreement.

These building blocks are widely held *core values* that seem to cross many boundaries of race, religion and philosophical bent. They also evidence a pretty keen foresight into the fundamental stuff of healthy matrimony.

In regard to core values, some matters are becoming more and more clear to me as I counsel soon-to-be married couples. Married couples can have different personalities and different hobbies and different histories. They can have different friends and different preferences and different opinions. But if they have divergent core values, there will be innumerable conflicts over almost every daily matter of life—time management, money management, sexual interplay, parenting, work and play. Divergent, even conflicting, core values create epicenters for relational earthquakes that can rock a marriage and shake our well-meant marriage vows to rubble.

So I keep asking. And I've added a few more questions like, "Do you both buy into this value?" And, "How is the trust basis of your relationship?" Or, "Do you see any rubs or harbor any worries that your list is different than his (or hers)?"

And in those hard moments when we detect some real potential friction, we tap the hammer gently with more careful questioning. In most cases, clarity brings understanding and mutual resolve to go forward. In a few instances, this conversation has created enough concern to give real pause.

It's not my job, generally speaking, to decide if couples should marry. Only once have I counseled a couple not to marry. Their values were so completely skewed from one another that I could not keep my peace. When they rebuffed my advice, I married them anyway. I'm not God. Neither am I a prophet. In that case, sadly, it didn't take divine or psychic perception to see the impending doom. Within months, that marriage ended.

Most of the couples I've married are still together today. Likely, some about whom I harbored private doubts are still going strong together. And likely, some that seemed to be "so together" have fallen apart.

Every ceremony includes a prayer that God will tie the knot tightly and perform a miracle: two becoming one. God can do this. The miracle does, of course, take some cooperation on the part of the betrothed. Marriage takes hard work and intentional effort. Few marriages are easy.

But when core values are shared, affirmed and exercised, marriages grow strong. The miracle has fertile soil in which to take form.

This book project began as a pre-marriage guide, preparing brides and grooms for happiness and health beyond the wedding. But as the work progressed, it became apparent that the need extended out to all couples, married and pre-married. I watched people near and dear to me struggle in their relationships and suffer through divorce. Even more, Sue and I steward our own stories of conflict and pain, resolution and growth. Twenty-seven years into marriage and ministry, I realize now more than ever that we all need good tools and ever-refined skills to keep our marriages fresh and forward moving.

Please understand—I'm still not an expert; I'm a student. I've been taking notes for a quarter of a century and I'm not about to stop now. It's time, though, to share some of my notes. More than the observations of premarriage novices, these notes do include more seasoned ones (mine and others').

I've also included many opportunities to "Stop, Talk and Listen." If you're working through this book as a couple—or as a group of couples—these questions deserve real consideration and brave honesty. The depth and quality of your experience might depend on these interactions. In some cases, these discussion starters simply won't apply to you. So just keep going and assume that very soon you'll hit one that opens a real can of worms. Some of these discussions will require courageous honesty.

How grateful I am that God has granted me the fellowship of the student in the seat next to mine. All of these pages, with some intimate revelations, are offered with the enthusiastic endorsement of my wife, Sue. Her commitment to the strength of our marriage "in sickness and in health" has been one of her many generous gifts. With great attention to detail, there are few things that Sue does halfheartedly. With considerable flair and care, Sue gift wraps my life.

We wish you the very best—an *unshakeable* marriage built on a sturdy set of core values. May God bless and strengthen you!

trust

It's such a naked feeling to share so much with you;
my heart, my body, my finances, my future.
Surely, you feel this risk, too.
I need to know that I'm safe with you.

Marriage is a giant step into vulnerability. In committing our lives to each other, we submit ourselves to innumerable risks for the sake of intimacy. We expose ourselves physically, emotionally, financially and completely to the influences of another.

For each individual, life is no longer confined to a simple cause-and-effect relationship between my decisions and the more random and distant effects of others around me. Now one other is granted the keys to my inner sanctuary. While I might guard certain privacies, even from my spouse, my life is not only an open book. Rather, it is a shared work—our stories will now be written onto the same pages.

For the best of reasons, we ordinarily welcome this. It seems that we've been created to live in interdependent relationships. We've been geared to enjoy intimacy. Most of us want deeply to love and be loved.

Despite the deep desire to love, there is risk. What if my love is not returned in fair measure? What if my private quirks and habits are grounds for rejection? What if my new partner has a closet of secrets that will tumble out on me when I un-wittingly open the door? All of us bring some insecurity into marriage.

Perhaps this insecurity explains the fact that trust is almost always the first *building block* that young couples list as a core value upon which to base a marriage. Amidst the queasy un-certainty of engagement, premarriage couples scramble to be the first to state the importance of trust. While pronouncing intent, they are also digging for reassurances: "Please tell me I can trust you."

STOP, TALK AND LISTEN

1. Marriage is risky business. I feel vulnerable. On a scale of one to ten, with one being the lowest and ten being the highest, this is where I feel the risk. (Circle and discuss.)

   Physical/Sexual Exposure   1 2 3 4 5 6 7 8 9 10

   Emotional Exposure   1 2 3 4 5 6 7 8 9 10

   Financial Exposure   1 2 3 4 5 6 7 8 9 10

   Another _____   1 2 3 4 5 6 7 8 9 10

2. I'm letting you peek into my private world. Soon, you'll be living in the middle of it. There are a few private things you should probably know (quirky habits, morning ritu-als, moody moments, secret sins).

My Past Matters

Maybe trust is so crucial because many people bring into mar-riage woeful tales of personal hurts and failed relationships. Many have been married previously and have suffered the trag-edy of divorce. With changing sexual mores, many have been involved in relationships confused by deep physical and roman-tic connectedness that are out of balance with shallow spiritual and friendship connections. Coming in and out of relationships, many have felt abandoned and betrayed—two strong negative experiences that rock us to the core. Still others bring stories of real abuse, both physical and mental, at the hands of those to whom they've bared themselves.

STOP, TALK AND LISTEN

My previous relationships have left their marks, for better or worse.

1. Discuss the relationships that have been most healthy.
2. Discuss the relationships that have been a mixture of good and bad.
3. Discuss the relationships that have left some residual pain. What are some ways your partner can help you to regain trust?
4. With regard to previous relationships, in what areas were you less than trustworthy?

Our Changing Culture

Perhaps most of all, commitments are not universally held in such sacred terms as in days past. People readily jump loyalties and dismiss covenants and contracts. All in all, people may not be as trusting, or as trustworthy, as in previous generations.

My parents and my wife's parents appear to have been driven by a core ethic—"Come hell or high water, we're in this together. Feelings and personal thrills are secondary in value compared to the higher call of commitment and personal convictions." Our parents stayed together through it all.

While our households of origin were not perfect, *our* values were shaped by *their* values. This helped my wife and me to trust each other. "Come hell or high water…."

But we're now in the minority—those raised in two-parent homes.

So as I approach the marriage ceremony, how do I trust that this person truly means "for better or worse"? What if our vows are a momentary wish born of shallow good intent? After all, I've watched friends (good people!) walk out on marriage, sometimes within a year. Why should I trust *this* person?

STOP, TALK AND LISTEN

1. Discuss your family's history in the realm of commitment. How did it affect you?
2. Were you ever shocked when someone close to you had a falling out? What did you learn from the experience?
3. What do you need from your partner to be reassured in the area of trust?

Little Trusts

So here come these young couples, brimming with hopes and fears. One pronounces the importance of trust in hopes that the other is equally determined to trust and be trustworthy. "Don't leave me hanging out here alone. I intend to bare myself to you. Please don't take advantage of me."

There are, of course, different kinds of trust. And not all matters of trust are equally dire. Some trusts, when broken, are easily repaired. If I tell my wife I'll be home at six o'clock, and then get home at seven for three nights in a row, trust is broken. She'll no longer believe me when I say I'll be home at six. But if I apologize, recommit and arrive home by six for ten days running, she'll likely call me a man of my word. Trust is repaired.

STOP, TALK AND LISTEN

1. Can you remember a time when you disappointed your partner?
2. Give your partner feedback; is he/she rekindling your trust? How?

The Big One

Sexual trust is a more daunting matter. And this is the trust that most young couples are speaking about when they leap to list trust as *building block number one.*

Sexuality, both literally and figuratively, strips us naked. It is a fiercely intimate act. We expose passions, noises, smells, hungers and physical quirks—all of this in an arena where most of us feel woefully inadequate. This is especially true as we try to compete with the flawless bodies and perfectly synchronized lovemaking of the stars in popular movies and magazines (all of whom benefit from multiple takes, makeup specialists, well-chosen camera angles and skilled editors).

Sex is, of course, one of God's greater gifts. The Creator could easily have made the reproductive act a chore as perfunctory as brushing our teeth. Instead, we are created to feel in sexual exchanges some of the most intense physical and emotional stimulation in all of life. Sex is good, particularly in the best context, spirit and proportion.

Sex is also intended to be a bonding agent. This most intimate exchange makes us feel intensely close to one another and, thus, intensely exposed to one another. When our highest highs happen in the arms of another, we are also vulnerable to our lowest lows. Our raw feelings are in the hands of another, for better or worse.

trust

19

When sexual trust is broken, the damage is virtually irreparable. I've known marriages that have survived a sexual break in trust. I've rarely known *trust* to survive a sexual break in trust. It appears to be a fracture that can seldom be reset. The marriage might go on, but it's likely to limp along without the many benefits of lasting trust.

STOP, TALK AND LISTEN

1. We'd all love to feel like a sexy movie personality when it's time to be intimate. This is probably closer to the truth:_____.
2. Sex should be a bonding agent in the marriage. Talk about the fears and hesitations that might make you hold back.
3. How can your partner be true to your trust? How do you think you'd feel if he/she wasn't?

The Benefits of Mutual Trust

What are the benefits of a lasting sexual trust? The benefit is the *freedom* to live my day, independent from my spouse, without fear that she is involved with another. And with that freedom comes worry-free focus on other matters. *Peace* and *confidence* mark the life of one unfettered by worries of compromised fidelity. Knowing that my spouse is loyal to me, I can fully enjoy and embrace the experiences that each day brings.

Respect is also a benefit of trust. As I trust my spouse, I also respect my spouse. She is being true to our vows, loyal to our intimate union, faithful to the process of what we are becoming together. And I feel her respect. She may be attracted to others. She might be tempted by certain situations. But her loyalty is a perpetual compliment. She has graced me with a central place in her life and I revel in her attentions. Her trustworthiness makes me feel special. I'm *the one* for her—and she for me.

For the sake of her freedom, peace, confidence and respect, I'm willing to go to great lengths. I don't want her to wonder for a moment about my loyalties. When I counsel women, I leave the door ajar or the curtains wide open. When I talk to other women apart from my wife, I won't allow conversations to become unduly intimate or physical proximity to be any different than it would be if my wife were present.

Yes, I'll hug a friend. And no, I haven't been able to avoid every potentially compromising situation. And yes, I have eyes to see attractive women and moments when I'm susceptible to their allure. Thus far, I've not had opportunity when I've been weak. And I've not been weak when I've had opportunity. God willing, ne'er the two shall meet. With God's help, I'll be true to the trust my wife has placed in me.

STOP, TALK AND LISTEN

1. On a scale of one to ten, this is how I feel when you're not with me:
   Freedom to engage with other matters
   1 2 3 4 5 6 7 8 9 10
   Peace about your involvements & relationships
   1 2 3 4 5 6 7 8 9 10
   Confidence in your ability to keep our sacred trust
   1 2 3 4 5 6 7 8 9 10
   Respect for how you handle other men/women
   1 2 3 4 5 6 7 8 9 10
2. To be honest, these settings are dangerous for me:

   _____.
3. I confess that I worry when you are with

   _____. Please help me to trust you.

Guarding Our Sacred Trust

Our trust is too valuable to break, so we must place guards, holds and speed bumps in our lives to keep us true. We need close friends in whom we can confide; friends strong enough to steer us back to our nobler instincts rather than merely sympathizing with our wanderlusts. We need to be part of a community that understands and upholds high standards. We need to fill our minds with things that are wholesome; matters that draw out the best in us rather than feeding the fires of our lesser impulses.

STOP, TALK AND LISTEN

1. As a couple, what are some practical ways that you can guard each other's trust?
2. Do you each have a confidante that you can tell almost anything to? If not, can you think of a person who could fill this role?
3. Which of your friends are not very helpful? Why?
4. Do you have adequate community or support structures to help you as a couple to maintain your high hopes?

Trust Is Risky Business

There are other exposures that require trust. We have to trust our spouses with joint bank accounts (finances are one of the most taxing issues on many marriages). We like to be able to trust our spouses with their portion of the parenting responsibilities. We want to trust them with our secrets, our things, our dreams. Ultimately, we want to trust that our spouses don't abuse the privilege of walking on sacred ground with access to priceless treasures.

Years ago, I was reaching out to a young man who had lost his father. I was trying to build a bridge of relationship. He was a baseball-card collector. I decided to open my treasure box. In a private place, I kept a cigar box filled with baseball and basketball cards from the 1960s. I had dozens of big-name cards, from a 1969 Nolan Ryan to a Lew Alcindor (later known as Kareem Abdul-Jabbar). The young man was so intrigued that I did the unthinkable. I let him take the box home.

Weeks later, I asked for the box. Months later, I was still asking for the box. Finally, the young man courageously admitted that he'd fallen prey to temptation. He'd sold several of my big-name cards.

I was devastated. Stealing from his pastor? It wasn't even about the money. It was about my memories, my heritage and my connection to childhood heroes!

Over time, the young man showed up with more than an apology. He brought some contemporary big-name cards for my collection. I received them with gratitude and tucked them in the cigar box, hardly noticing the names. I shut the box and didn't open it for many years. It was too painful. I'd forgiven the young man. But I'd never forget the disillusionment. And I hadn't forgiven myself for being so trusting.

One day, I decided to open the box. I was no longer angry. I wasn't even overly curious. It was just a whim. I wondered what cards he had given me.

Sitting on the very top of the pile was a Mark McGuire rookie card. At the time the boy gave me the baseball card, Mark McGuire was a highly regarded power-hitter with decent numbers. At the moment I *found* the card, Mark McGuire had just broken Roger Maris's single-season home run record. The card was worth hundreds, maybe thousands of dollars. The experience was priceless. Even though my trust had been broken, I believe that God rewarded my vulnerability and willingness to risk for the sake of relationship.

Given enough time, coupled with the astounding choreography of God, most hurts get healed. And there are always new treasures to share together and enjoy. Would I open my box to another? Can I trust again? Of course. Why not? Intimacy is worth it. To trust and to be found trustworthy are noble values.

But trust is also fragile and must be guarded. Humans are capable of great allegiance and great treachery. Marriage is the ultimate testing ground for the trustworthiness of our character. Many other *building blocks* actually rest on this one.

STOP, TALK AND LISTEN

1. "I want to trust you with our children and I want you to trust me." Discuss any fear you have in this area.
2. Have you ever been gravely disappointed when you trusted someone? Tell your partner about it.
3. Is there anything else your partner should know about your trustworthiness?

"What Ifs" and "What Abouts"

My partner's parents have been divorced. Does this mean that my partner is more likely to pull the plug on our covenant?

Statistically, yes. Because children of divorce have found the experience to be awful but survivable, they might be more likely to inflict it upon their own loved ones. And the "how to" of trust and loyalty has not been modeled in their family of origin. So, yes, there is a greater statistical possibility of divorce in these cases.

But people are not statistics. Get this issue out in the open and *really* talk. Some children of divorce are fanatics about loyalty because of the hardships they've experienced. Our previous pains sometimes drive us to an opposite extreme from the things we've suffered.

My partner has been divorced. Does this make my partner more likely to pull the plug?

Again, statistically, yes. People who have divorced are more likely to divorce again. Why? Because they survived the first one. They'll survive again, if need be.

But again, a person is not a statistic. I know many people who have learned from the first marriage (and divorce) and have successful and lasting relationships afterward. Again, this topic deserves a lot of mutual conversation.

My partner is absentminded and inattentive to details—finances, household chores, being on time, picking up things at the store. Will I go through life without any trust in his/her ability to follow through?

People grow. People learn and improve. But don't bank on it, and don't marry this person for who he/she might become. If it drives you crazy now, it will push you to the limits later. If you become a nag, you'll push your partner to the limit.

Yes, you can trust this person ... to be altogether imperfect. The key question is whether these lapses are truly absentmindedness or rather passive-aggressive behavior. If it's the latter, then you're not marrying someone who is forgetful. You're marrying someone who is angry. This should be flushed out.

Can trust be rebuilt?

Little trusts get repaired and rebuilt all the time. The bigger the trust, risk, and seriousness of the matter at hand, the more time and help will be necessary to rebuild trust. As for sexual trust, it takes a miracle from God to rebuild. I've heard testimonies of that kind of miracle, but choose not to put God to a foolish test.

CHAPTER 2

communication

With every available tool, including words,
can we prove our interest and deepen our understanding
so that life together can be a pleasure?

Good communication breeds intimacy. Good communication promotes understanding. Good communication conveys its own set of messages—mutual regard and keen interest in one another. Communication is a building block of a strong marriage.

Poor communication creates distance. Poor communication transmits its own set of messages. In the passive sense, poor communication imparts disregard and disinterest. In a more aggressive sense, poor communication indicates hostility or even enmity. A lack of good communication leads to tensions and fault lines that will shake a household to pieces.

As I pen these words, I'm watching three men build a wrought-iron fence. The voice of the grouchy boss is echoing around the courtyard of the outdoor café where I often write. He under-communicates instruction to the other two workers and he over-communicates his correction. He refuses to grant affirmation and readily casts insults. If his eyes are warmer than his words, they are hidden behind sunglasses.

The two workers appear timid, afraid to make mistakes and terribly sorry to be here. To make matters worse, one of the workers speaks no English and the other has to play the interpreter. Frankly, I'm glad it's not my fence they're building. More than that, I have little hope for the potential of an enduring relationship between this boss and his employees.

This fence-building scenario illustrates a point: marriage needs hope to survive, and any real hope for sticking together requires good communication. Both partners need to own this value—communication matters, a lot.

STOP, TALK AND LISTEN

1. Describe communication in your household of origin. A lot of talk or only a bit? Rowdy and raucous or reserved and subdued?
2. How do you feel about the overall quality of communication in your relationship?
3. Do you both seem to own the value of strong, clear communication?

Use Your Words

The most obvious form of communication is verbal. Words help.

Anyone with a toddler knows how desperately they want to be understood. Toddlers often express frustration when we can't understand the need they feel so intensely. We say phrases like, "Use your words," so that they will discover and exercise the enormous potential in their growing vocabulary to communicate feelings and wants.

Sometimes, adults act like toddlers. We fuss and groan and cry and withdraw and punish and slam cupboards because a spouse cannot understand or respond to our feelings or needs. Often, we haven't used words. We've forgotten to explain ourselves, or else we've failed to listen to each other.

There is simply no substitute for sitting down face-to-face and talking; or lying down side by side and talking; or walking hand in hand and talking—with active, attentive listening. The goal, by the way, of any form of communication is mostly understanding; but good communication also fosters clarity, perspective, honesty and respect.

STOP, TALK AND LISTEN

1. How frequently do you feel misunderstood by your partner?
2. Do either or both of you assume that the other person can read minds, or "should know" without having to be told?

Men, Women and the Volume of Words

In the stereotypical marriage, the woman does more talking than the man. Studies indicate that this stereotype proves true in the greater number of marriages. Deborah Tannen notes that while men talk more and longer in public, women talk more in the home. "For many men, the home means freedom from having to prove themselves and impress through verbal display … they are free to remain silent. But for women, home is a place where they are free to talk, and where they feel the greatest need for talk, with those they are closest to."[1]

So, men, this means learning to listen. It even means learning to probe for more information, sometimes in moments when you feel as if you have quite enough information already. Or, if the frustration of overload is too much, learning to say, "I'm having difficulty processing all of the information you've given me. Help me to understand" this part or that part.

Women, this might mean slowing down or easing up, or making sure the dialogue is more equitable. He might need you to probe a bit for his feelings and views, even though he's likely to resist at first. He definitely needs to trust you with his feelings, or he'd rather not reveal them.

---

1 Deborah Tannen, *You Just Don't Understand: Women and Men in Conversation* (New York: William-Morrow Publishers), 1990.

communication

Men, she wants you to open up. She likely finds intimacy through the exchange of personal information. You might identify your closest friend as "the person I can sit quietly with for hours without having to say a thing." But this is absolutely not true for your wife. Her closest friends are probably the ones she exchanges secrets and stresses and lamentations with. Deborah Tannen calls it "troubles talk" and notes that "bonding through troubles is widespread among women and common between women and men. It seems to be far less common between men." [2]

Of course, this also begs the question about intimacy as a shared value. Please be honest with each other. Some people really don't want to get very close. For others, a lack of intimacy in marriage is nonsensical. But assuming that closeness is a shared value, good communication requires that men (and women) actually talk, and that women (and men) use words well. Tannen writes:

> Women tend to show understanding of another woman's feelings. When men try to reassure women by telling them that their situation is not so bleak, the women hear their feelings being belittled or discounted. Again, they encounter a failure of intimacy just when they were bidding to reinforce it. [3]

Men, on the other hand, believe that we are doing each other a favor when we diminish and dismiss woes. In our minds, we're adding a bit of needed perspective that will contribute to the resolution of the issue.

2 Ibid.
3 Ibid.

STOP, TALK AND LISTEN

1. Who talks more and how much? Talk honestly about the percentage breakdown in your relationship.
2. How does the other feel about being the more frequent listener?
3. Define intimacy and talk about the degree to which each of you believes that verbal interplay is important.
4. Talk to each other about your other "best friends." What makes them "best"?

Say the Right Things the Right Way

If we're going to talk, we might as well talk *well*. This means learning to say the things that should be said in the best manner possible.

Some families just blurt everything out with volumes and tones and levels of obtuse truth that other families would view as hostile. Insults fly. Emotions soar. Debates break out.

Some families are more careful, living according to guardian phrases like, "If you can't say something nice, don't say anything at all."

Strangely, we often mate according to a subtle longing to escape the extremes of the system employed in our households of origin. Someone from the Loud Family will often marry someone from the Nice Family. The one seeks relief from harsh overcommunication, the other from constipated undercommunication in their households of origin.

But when we marry, we carry the blessings and foibles of our pasts with us. We expect and assume that others won't trod all over "our way." When we're dating, it seems cute to have a potential spouse who is "so refreshingly different." But once the new and united household takes form, the natural assumption is that it will take form in "my way." The spouse from the Loud Family will want spirited and wide-open communication, even if that desire is subconscious. The spouse from the Nice Family will subtly hope for peace and quiet at all cost.

communication

Of course, sometimes we're so determined to break out of our pasts that we hyperextend to the opposite pole. Still, the challenge is before us to find ways of communicating that *actually work*. This is rarely a "better or best" decision between extremes. Rather, it's a dynamic journey to discover what actually works for us.

As a whole, of course, gentleness, honesty, sympathy, empathy, courage and self-control work best. These are the better parts of each gene pool. Words can do so much damage. Words can do so much good. Yes, some couples "nice" themselves to death. But more often, people are simply too mean and nasty. It almost always pays (as we tell our children) to talk nice. Or as the Bible puts it, "[speak] the truth in love."[4] And in the book of Proverbs it says, "A word aptly spoken is like apples of gold in settings of silver."[5]

STOP, TALK AND LISTEN

1. Again, talk about your households of origin. How did your families talk to each other? Loudly or quietly? Through controversy or avoidance? Gentle and tactful or harsh and direct?
2. Now, tell each other the truth about the "tone" you prefer in the home you are building together.
3. Does either of you react or respond badly to a particular communication style?
4. Do you own the same commitment to telling the truth in love? Why or why not?

Giving Verbal Cues

Sometimes, the simplest verbal cue can derail a menacing conflict or lend understanding where there's been only confusion.

---

4 Ephesians 4:15.
5 Proverbs 25:11.

"I need to tell you something that's hard to hear. Are you ready for it?" This gives the listener a chance to brace, or even to delay when necessary, so the hard word can be received and processed. "You asked, but do you really want to know how I feel about this?" Such words allow the other to honestly measure whether listening and understanding are possible, versus one-way purging or spouting.

"You need to know that I'm very tired right now, so I can't guarantee I'll be very good at dialogue." This simple spoken acknowledgment could rescue hundreds of couples from hundreds of painful conflicts that would never have erupted if they'd chosen to cover a hard topic after helpful rest.

"For some reason, I feel a need for some space tonight." A clear expression of honest emotion, this cue opens the door for the other to say, "Good, I'll try to give you that space," or else to say, "I'm feeling the opposite need. How can we help each other?" Either way, the lines of communication are open, instead of clumsily disappointing each other or colliding in hurtful ways.

These cues—there are thousands of potential ones—simply help so much. They work for people who talk more and even more for people who talk less. These cues help us to understand each other in the moment and, really, to dance the dance of life without constantly stepping on each other. Find a set of cues that work for you.

The bottom line is not to assume the other person needs no cues. This dance is sophisticated. Begin to practice this fine art.

Similar to the verbal cue is the sandwich approach. *This involves "sandwiching" hard truth between affirmations or encouragements so the harder thing is more palatable.* Give the partner time to process this information and respond in a seasoned way.

STOP, TALK AND LISTEN

1. Can you think of a time when a "verbal cue" did help or might have helped?
2. Talk about the value of verbal cues. Do they help "soften the blow of hard truth"?
3. How are you at using the "sandwich approach" to hard truth (sandwiching the hard part between affirmations or encouragements)?

Ouch! That Hurts!

If "a word aptly spoken is like apples of gold in settings of silver,"[6] then ugly words are like crab apples with mold in settings of sulphur. Fine words build up. Ugly words tear down.

Sarcasm is one nasty use of language that can eat away at trust and friendship. Sarcasm can be a playful friendship-builder when we're harmlessly teasing or when both participate in the banter. But when sarcasm licks with flames of anger and disrespect, it burns. The other partner will become cautious if communications are tainted with scorn or disdain.

Putdowns will accomplish exactly what the word implies. They put the other person down instead of building that person up. All of us need to find constructive ways to voice criticism, and putdowns are not constructive. Avoid the word "You . . ." at the beginning of any sentence and much hardship will be avoided. Learn to say, "When _____ happens, this is how it makes me feel." Non-accusative "I" language is one of the true arts of healthy relating.

Avoid "you always" or "you never," which are rarely accurate and often overloaded with accusation. Try, "When_____ happens often, it makes me feel _____."

---

6 Proverbs 25:11.

And name-calling kills. The marks and images left by name-calling and verbal assault are difficult to live down. Those insults can be forgiven, but they are rarely forgotten. Negative names continue to bounce around in our minds, jabbing at our self-esteem and undermining intimacy.

STOP, TALK AND LISTEN

1. How are you with sarcasm? Does it sting your relationship or do you like the banter?
2. Do either of you feel put down too frequently? Talk about it.
3. Do you always say "always"? Or do you never say "never"?
4. Have there been any names thrown at you that have left scars, either by your partner or someone else?

A Picture Is Worth a Thousand Words

Visual cues impart almost as much information as words. Occasionally, they tell more. Sometimes, gestures and countenance tell the truth when words lack authenticity. Too often, we just don't think about nonverbal cues and remain ignorant about the ways they either aid or disrupt good communication.

Most obviously, nonverbal communication involves a sophisticated set of expressions which supplement our vocabulary. We add nuances of meaning or relative importance to our words when we wave our hands, scrunch our faces, stand up straight, arch our backs, fold our arms, pop our knuckles, wring our hands, shift from one foot to the other, tap our toes, pound our fists, point our fingers, turn our backs, wag our heads, purse our lips, curl our lips, squint our eyes, roll our eyes, set our jaws, smile with scorn, smile with positive regard or otherwise exercise some secondary body part to communicate thought or feeling.

Some people give off cold nonverbal cues. They may not intend to put people off, and might even suffer loneliness without

communication

knowing why. The reason? Non-verbals say "no," or "stay away" or "I don't really like you," or "just try to be nice to me!"

Other people have warm, inviting nonverbals. They say, "Yes" without saying a word.

Sometimes our body language betrays us. A spouse might say, "I love you," but doesn't realize that negative gestures are creating double messages. I used to tell my wife, "I'd love to spend the day shopping with you," and then prove myself duplicitous with yawn after slouch after roll of the eyes, all creating terrible confusion for my wife. An activity that I intended for intimacy created tension.

So we need to learn some things. Open arms and open smiles invite interaction. Folded arms and closed facial expressions beg for space (unless the folding of the arms is a generous decision to put a shy person at ease by being less intrusive and more respectful of space). Closing the spacial gap is an overture of relational interest. Widening that gap is a show of caution or disinterest. Physical touch is generally endearing, unless another person truly reacts badly to it. Study someone's face *in repose*. An introvert will likely have a countenance that says, "I'm gathering energy. Please leave me alone for a while until I'm refueled." An extrovert will likely have a countenance that says, "Come close to me and be my friend. I have time and energy for you."

This is not to make you self-conscious; only self-aware. Why? For the sake of clear communication.

STOP, TALK AND LISTEN

1. Can you think of ways you or your partner "betray yourself" with gestures or expressions?
2. Help each other understand your propensities for body language. Now consider where you learned these devices.
3. Do any non-verbal cues need to be relearned or unlearned?

Actions Speak Louder Than Words

To some people, their word is their seal. To others, words are only words until they are proven. To all of us, words lose their power when actions override their meaning and value. Consider the following exchange:

"You said you care about me! You say you think of me all the time! But you also said you'd be home at six o'clock, and it's seven-thirty!"

"But something came up."

"Something more important than me?"

"Of course not. Something more urgent."

"There is always something more urgent than keeping your promises. How can I believe anything you say?"

And so goes this all-too-common argument.

Truth be told, actions tell truth better than words. I say that I love you. Fine, but do I treat you in loving ways? I say that I care about your feelings, wishes and preferences. Fine, but do I give them priority? I say that you're the most important person in my life. Fine, but do I give the boss or my parents or friends—no matter how worthy of interest—more authority to gather, hold or hijack my attention?

Our actions say things that words fall short of saying. Actions are the most critical form of communication. And our inaction speaks volumes. Some people communicate active disinterest or subtle rebellion by exercising passive-aggressive behavior. That phrase (which will be used several times in this book) means that our inaction can be a show of anger.

STOP, TALK AND LISTEN

1. You've seen the "classic" argument example. Is it familiar to either of you?
2. Are there any empty words in your relationship—emotional declarations or promises that lack follow-through?
3. Which comes easier to each of you—actions or words? Why?

Do You Tend to Communicate Thoughts or Feelings?

The Myers-Briggs Personality Test uses thinker/feeler as a primary personality distinctive. It doesn't measure whether you can think or feel. It does indicate which you give preference or authority to.

Gary Smalley states that "In roughly 80% of all homes, men primarily relate to their wives using what we call a language of the head while women tend to speak a language of the heart."[7] It doesn't surprise me that the greater majority of women tend to be "feelers," giving their emotional considerations and reactions greater influence. In fact, women tend to start sentences that involve opinion or conviction by saying, "I feel that...." This doesn't imply that women don't or can't think as well as men. It simply means that feelings trump rational considerations more often than not.

As most imagine, the greater portion of men are "thinkers." This means that more men tend to give greater authority to rational thought (pros and cons, cost-benefit analysis) drawing from research, experience or from other authorities more than from feelings. Thinkers do, of course, feel a great deal. But emotion is

7 Gary Smalley, "Communication: The Language of Love," December 28, 2004, www.smalleyonline.com/articles/m_communication.html.

mistrusted and devalued by many "thinkers." Feelings carry less internal authority. Most often, men begin to communicate an opinion or conviction by saying, "Well, I think that...."

This leads to potential conflict. Men—not all, or always—tend to look for rational solutions to complex issues. Women—not all, or always—tend toward the expression of feeling and the solicitation of sympathy—not solutions—when faced with complexity.

Women frequently communicate frustration when "He won't listen! He only wants to try to fix things. He's so insensitive!"

Men, predictably, communicate irritation because "She won't listen to reason or common-sense solutions. She just wants to wallow in her emotions!"

Simply understanding these distinctions can spare couples a lot of frustration. This is not a better or worse categorization. It should seem obvious that by validating emotion, feelers draw out the very real and deeply felt matters of the heart that thinkers tend to ignore to their own detriment. And thinkers bring a healthy dose of reason and rationale to feelers who are too often swamped or stunted by the power of their emotions.

In other words, this difference is good, and we usually (not always) marry someone who possesses the other quality. This is one case where opposites attract and when we truly can "complete" one another.

Again, the key is understanding each other. Knowing each others' proneness to communicate out of deep emotion or rational thought helps sidestep misunderstanding.

STOP, TALK AND LISTEN

1. If you've never taken a Myers-Briggs test, try to arrange for one. They are remarkably accurate and useful.
2. Are you a feeler? Do you understand that your partner might discount his/her own feelings in favor of rational consideration?
3. Are you a thinker? Do you understand that your partner might discount his/her rational thought in favor of deep feelings?
4. Are you okay with your differences? If so, how so? If not, where is the snag?

"What Ifs" and "What Abouts"

What if I am ready to marry someone who is mean with words—even verbally abusive?

Put the marriage on hold. No one should have to live this life with a verbal bully. Almost everyone, of course, blows up and flips out—some more than others. But if there is little self-awareness or proactive energy given toward real change, please spare yourself a very sad life.

Try communicating your concern in "I" language. "I'm not eager, or even willing, to endure harsh words in our marriage. My hope is that together we can find ways to talk that aren't destructive. Can we do this together?" Obviously, much more must be said, but that's a start.

What if I'm already married and I'm getting verbally pounded?
Get help. Get strong, with the help of God and any resource available. Don't let your own health be tied solely to your spouse's ability to speak nicely to you. Then, using every kind of persuasion, make sure your spouse has tools available to learn new skills or constraints.

If your spouse won't or can't change, seek a therapist who shares your values to help you navigate these hard waters. Have hope. Many people do change and intimacy is saved whenever verbal assailants submit to a pathway toward health and growth.

What if my spouse just won't talk? It's like I'm the only one doing all the work!
Again, communicate your concerns in "I" language. "Sometimes I feel as if our communication is one-way. It makes me feel disconnected, lonely and frustrated."

Then give your spouse a chance to think, talk and respond. Don't try to speed or manipulate this process. You might learn something quite valuable from waiting on a seasoned response.

I'm a bad listener. How do I get better? It seems like I'm always preparing my next comment.
Everyone has different pacing, and some people naturally interrupt as part of the flow of conversation. This is not always rude and can lead to some spicy, rich interaction. Pay attention to quiet people. If they never speak, it's possible that you talk too much and listen too little. It's also possible that your partner simply needs more space and less overlapping as conversation is paddled back and forth.

I'm married to a woman who rarely, if ever, interrupts or forces her way into a group conversation. When I'm with her, I'm learning to slow way down and try, try, try to allow her enough pauses so that she can get some momentum up. Once she does, look out. I'm the rich beneficiary of her marvelous stories, humor, insight and deeply felt opinions. Most others will know her as "that amazing listener" and will wonder after

communication

41

every meeting why they talked so much. Truthfully, they didn't pause enough to allow her time to formulate a response.

My partner thinks I should read minds. What do I do?
Simply rehearse your probing skills. "Tell me what your hopes are for tonight." Or, "What's something that I could do to make your day better?" Or, "Is there anything that a good cup of coffee (face-to-face) could help with?" Beat your partner to the punch. Anticipate. Ask. Care!

My partner shuts me down; he/she doesn't listen or care how I feel. What do I do?
Use "I" language: "Sometimes I feel shut out, or like I talk and no one is listening. Am I accurate? Is there something I need to know about what I'm saying or making you feel?"

Now get ready for an honest answer and it might not be flattering. Maybe your spouse is bored by too much detail, or overwhelmed by so much feeling. Or your partner might be frustrated by "same old, same old" patterns and feels helpless. Remember, women, most men go crazy listening to problems without want of solutions. You might consider asking for ten minutes to explain and emote and then actually invite some insights and advice. That last piece will help your husband feel like he's more engaged in the process and that his input is valuable.

I don't trust my spouse with my emotions. Either they get thrown back at me, or ridiculed, or spread to other people, or they land heavily on my spouse and create stress. It's better to just hold it all in, or tell someone who is objective and removed.
Again, try the "I" language: "When I share feelings, I feel vulnerable. It's hard for me to trust. How can I be sure my sharing won't be managed badly?" Communicate your willingness to be more forthcoming, as long as there is a reciprocal desire to be a good caretaker of shared information. Communicate your hopes: "This is what I'm hoping for when I open up." Be very explicit. Your partner will likely appreciate some direction, as long as you haven't gotten accusative.

CHAPTER 3

commitment

You're stuck with me, for better or worse.
I'm in this 'til death do us part.
This is a decision I've made and life will not shake it loose.

In the marriage ceremony, everyone recites virtually the same words: "For better, for worse; for richer, for poorer; in sickness and in health; to love and to cherish, 'til death do us part." We call them "vows." They represent a sacred covenant "before God and these witnesses."

So what's the problem? Why do half of all marriages in America fail? Why are these words losing their "pop," their "stick," their staying power? Well, for one thing, marriage can be difficult. Even for the most affectionate partners, conflict and hurt and loss and change and so many factors can make it hard to hold to our vows—especially in difficult seasons.

But, still, there is this matter of commitment. It simply means persevering no matter how hard it gets.

In the premarriage process, virtually everyone says the same thing. "I'm in this for the long haul. No matter what happens or how I feel, I can't walk out on this marriage." Frankly, if anyone didn't say that, I'd refuse to officiate at the wedding. So far, I haven't refused anyone, though a few have refused me when they have heard my values and requirements for marital preparation.

So why don't people *mean it* when they say "no matter what?" Probably, most *do* mean it. More than that, there is some naïveté about how hard this covenant really can be to keep. Others devalue their vows because God doesn't have legitimate or authentic authority—we hold a very soft theology of God. Still others simply believe that if they aren't happy, divorce is excusable and preferable.

STOP, TALK AND LISTEN

1. Do you believe you are getting married for life?
2. Are you prepared to work hard, see a counselor and do whatever it takes if life requires it?

But What About …?

Let me pause to acknowledge that even the Bible (Jesus himself) authorizes divorce in cases of marital infidelity. [8] The Bible doesn't *recommend* divorce, since the core of Christian truth is all about forgiveness and second chances. But there seems to be an acknowledgment that sexual infidelity breaks the bond of marriage in a deep and grievous way. It's understandable that this profound disruption of the marital covenant can create an irreparable condition.

Then there is physical abuse. In most cases, pastors or counselors recommend—at least—therapeutic separation until one or both partners can participate in long-term counseling and rage management training. Sometimes the offending partner refuses. I would never tell someone that he or she is locked into a longsuffering relationship with a violent person.

---

8 Matthew 5:32.

As for verbal or emotional abuse, it has become the easy way out—the quick and simple justification for anyone to walk out on a marriage. "He's verbally abusive!" "She emotionally assaults me every day." This might be true. If a pastor or counselor can assess real, honest-to-goodness abuse is taking place, it might be good to separate and find serious help. And if one person won't get help, that seems to be a form of abandonment that some people would say "breaks covenant." While the Bible paints longsuffering as an admirable trait, I can't imagine God asking us to stay in a marriage in which a partner pounds away at us verbally or emotionally without remorse or any effort toward change. But, frankly, most marriages have seasons or events where the language gets heated and heavy. If that were grounds for divorce, few people would stay married. Better to find help and learn new conflict management skills than walk out.

Often, the relationship just springs a leak and loses luster. Lost affection and unresolved differences make the marriage totally unsatisfying. This is *not* grounds for divorce and is typical of almost every marriage at one time or another. This is the kind of reality we must learn to ride out and grow through together.

In a few cases, one partner withholds intimacy. Even though that behavior is a potent corrosive for a marriage, one that goes directly against the teaching of the Bible, it is my opinion that this form of emotional and sexual abandonment is not grounds for divorce. Obviously, others will disagree, but I simply don't see evidence in the Bible—my primary source for counsel and authority—that this kind of withholding legitimizes divorce.

Here is the simple counsel of Christian Scripture: God hates divorce. It is forgivable, but absolutely foreign to God's intention.

STOP, TALK AND LISTEN

1. Are there conditions in which you can imagine walking away from a marriage?
2. If you had a friend who is unhappy in a dry or angry marriage, what advice would you give?

More Than Merely Us

In our "me-istic" culture, we are too wrapped up in self and our own private affairs. We think the only victims of marital failure are the couple. That is simply not true.

Divorce damages children. Hardly a study in the world suggests that children are "better off because of divorce than they would be in a strained marriage." No, they usually are not.

Divorce damages culture. The breakdown of the family unit creates enormous friction and complex societal challenges that cost everyone in numerous ways—from the cost of legal proceedings, to custody issues, to therapeutic cleanup, to the cost of crime and prisons, where a terrible percentage of inmates are children of divorce. For example, 70% of incarcerated juveniles come from single-parent homes and 53% of all inmates in prisons come from a home without a father.[9]

And, obviously, children of divorce are far less likely to have successful, lasting relationships in the future. So this problem has exponential potential for harm.

Spiritually, marriage is supposed to be a model of the unique covenant relationship that Christ has with the church. Our marriages are different, of course, because both contributors to the covenant are imperfect. But the Bible teaches that we are to "submit to one another out of reverence for Christ."[10]

9 U.S. Department of Justice 2002.
10 Ephesians 5:21.

It teaches that a wife is submissive to her husband as if he were Jesus; and that the husband loves his wife the way Jesus loved the church "by giving himself up for her." This mutual servanthood and extreme loyalty is supposed to be a daily reminder of Christ, who came "not . . . to be served, but to serve" and to lay down his life.[11] The biblical model of marriage is not male-dominant. It is Christ-inspired. So when people see this picture—this paradigm—come undone, they see a tragedy of heavenly proportions. The model is ripped to shreds and a fundamental purpose for marriage is thwarted.

STOP, TALK AND LISTEN

1. Are you a child of divorce? How has it affected you? (If not, do you know others?)
2. If marriage is a building block of society, and commitment is a building block of marriage, how is failed marital commitment hurting society?

Where Do You Come From?

So, what if you are a child of divorce?

It's time for some soul-searching. If you've survived divorce, it's possible (even likely?) that you will subtly minimize the seriousness of divorce and the sacredness of your vows. Why? Because, though wretched, divorce in the family was survivable. For many children of divorce (and often individuals who themselves have been previously divorced), there is a natural "eject" lever that makes it more plausible to say, "I'm out of here!" when things get too heated or too hard. While divorce sounds painful, it is proven to be survivable.

---

11 Mark 10:45.

commitment

I grew up in a home where my parents' imperfect marriage lasted until death pulled them apart. My wife grew up in a home where her parents' imperfect marriage has lasted for more than half a century. For us, imperfect marriage is the norm, and holding an imperfect marriage together is virtually a given. While in the midst of conflict, we've certainly been tempted to cut and run. We might even have threatened to do so! But that was never really an option. All that is true, at least in part, because of what our parents modeled. We want to honor them for this blessed legacy.

While our marriage is bolstered by many positive ingredients, we would both describe our relationship as having been "highly conflictual" in particular seasons. All that to say, divorce isn't in our vocabulary, even though we've hurt each other deeply at times. When we spoke our vows, we assumed that we'd live and love together until death, and we assume that to this day. There is simply no "eject lever" in our thinking.

Does this mean that children of divorce are destined to divorce? Should grown children of successful marriages avoid marrying children of divorce?

Of course not. But there has to be some hard thinking, deep praying and honest talking. Again, *family of origin* issues really do matter.

STOP, TALK AND LISTEN

1. If divorce can predispose divorce, what can a person or couple do to offset this?
2. Some people are far more determined to make it work because they've been hurt by those who didn't. Have you seen other friends or family members give up on marriage? What happened?

"What Ifs" and "What Abouts"

What if I'm about to marry someone who doesn't value commitment the way I do?

Do the hard thing. Cancel the wedding. This is a virtual guarantee —at some point the marriage will become very difficult. Chances are very good that your partner will leave you.

What if I'm already married to someone who doesn't share my core value toward commitment?

Communicate your concerns using "I" language. For example, "I feel vulnerable because it seems as if commitment is not an equally shared value." If this is a genuine divergence, get counseling now from a marriage therapist who shares your values. If you don't know of a therapist who shares your values, your pastor will.

What if I don't own this value? What if commitment is too scary or too much for me?

If you aren't married, either find a thoughtful helper (counselor, friend, pastor) to explore the reasons for being skittish about commitment, or else don't marry. Commit to living a single life and don't inflict your inability to commit onto another person's well-being.

What if I really am miserable but have no seemingly legitimate grounds for divorce?

Get help. Get well. Try to encourage your partner to participate in your marital wellness. Stay married. Don't base your personal wellness on the other person's ability to make you happy. And don't go to divorced friends to be your helpers and confidantes. A few divorced friends will say, "Don't do it. It hurts too much. Stay in your marriage." Most, in my experience, will easily and often show you exit strategies. And don't rely only on family. They will almost always give you subjective, slanted input and will likely be wearing blinders regarding the matters that make you miserable. Your spouse might not be the sole issue. It could be you! Or depression. Or some other sad reality that must be dealt with.

Are there signs I should be looking for in a spouse; especially in regard to commitment?

Yes. Don't marry a quitter. Don't marry someone who quits teams, jobs, tasks or friendships too readily. That predisposition to quitting is a scary predictor.

And if your partner has no God-consciousness, or no sense of responsibility or accountability to a higher moral authority than personal preference, look out. Yes, there are principled and loyal atheists and agnostics, but people who are highly committed to God are much less likely than others to walk out on a marriage.

CHAPTER 4

compromise

I'll come your way. I respect you that much.
If you can do the same we'll make this work.

Compromise is a very common *building block* in the minds of premarried couples. It's as if they're fresh in the middle of counting the costs and making the adjustments necessary to strike this initial bargain. It feels unnatural, quite awkward and they hope to grow into it.

Be encouraged. Healthy marriages are marked by a steady stream of compromises, adaptations, gives and takes—and it all ends up being quite natural for those who aren't entirely self-absorbed.

But know this—self-absorption, self-centeredness and any form of selfishness have to be laid (in principle) at the altar on the day of the wedding. Marriage gets really hard and ugly if boorish, spoiled, bratty, self-involved people are unwilling to learn a better way. If I'm someone who insists on my own way, I'm going to make my partner very unhappy, and I'll likely join that pitiful party.

Jesus is the best teacher on this topic. As the story goes in the second chapter of the book of Philippians, he came to earth relinquishing any need to keep a tight grip on his own authority as God's son.[12] He emptied himself of pride and position, entered our world as a human baby and became a servant—giving, giving, giving.

And receiving, of course. His approach to life was so winsome that people adored him, respected him and followed his model. The ones afraid to relinquish power were threatened by this radical way of life. But Jesus' manner of thinking and living has taken hold, and his apprentices number in the billions —both today and over the centuries.

So how do we do this—how do we learn to compromise? You might imagine that I recommend a crash course in Jesus 101. Read the biblical books of Matthew, Mark, Luke and John. You'll see an approach to life and love that would virtually guarantee a rewarding marriage if even one half of Jesus' teachings were integrated.

STOP, TALK AND LISTEN

1. Are you a stubborn person or a flexible, compromising person?
2. How do you see each other? C'mon, honestly?
3. How familiar are you with the model of Jesus? Does his approach to life guide you in any way?

Compromise Is Pretty Good, Pretty Much

The downside of compromise, of course, is that no one gets completely what he or she hopes for. Compromise involves borrowing pieces and parts of each partner's hopes or finding a third alternative. Either way, things don't turn out the way either person had hoped. Sometimes a better way is forged, but most often there's a loss involved.

---

12 Philippians 2:6-8.

So what's so good about compromise? Demonstrating respect for the other person. Finding a peaceable solution to divergent wants. Proving your willingness to bend in order to serve and build consensus and unity.

STOP, TALK AND LISTEN

1. Can you think of a time when compromise was totally helpful in getting you past an impasse?
2. Can you think of a time when compromise was not entirely satisfying?
3. Are you emotionally prepared to compromise a lot? Where are you a holdout?

Too Little, Too Much

Some people refuse to compromise and seem proud of their inflexibility. This can be a strong trait when it's applied to a matter of moral conscience or societal good. But it can also be a terrible drag on a relationship when someone turns every little issue into a matter of staunch principle. Worse yet is the person who simply has no self-awareness about the constant need to be right, or to have personal wants consistently satisfied.

On the other extreme, some people concede far too much. They become doormats and dishrags, always giving but never receiving. This can seem so noble, but it leads to damaged marriages and misguided martyrdom.

Jesus taught self-giving love, but he was no martyr. Even his death on the cross was fully anticipated and absolutely courageous. Jesus spoke truth, even hard truth, to the people who plotted his death. However flimsy he looks in some tired old artwork, Jesus was a construction worker—a man's man and no pushover.

compromise

How can you be self-giving *and* strong? By communicating your hopes with clarity and giving your spouse every opportunity to *also* be strong by self-giving. The best marriages are like dancing. There's a reciprocity and a mutuality that invites both partners to step into something that is truly noble, each taking the lead at times as an act of service and letting the other lead by serving.

STOP, TALK AND LISTEN

1. Compromise is fine, but what if only one plays the game? How would that feel to you?
2. Have you ever seen someone who is utterly inflexible in a marriage just wear the other person out?
3. Do you lean toward being a controller or toward being a pushover? What do you intend to do about these attitudes *together*?

Give and Take—Still a Better Way

Give and take works better than compromise. It allows the possibility that sometimes I get *exactly* what I'm hoping for. It guarantees that sometimes my partner gets *exactly* what she's hoping for. And, it communicates so much respect!

Note that *give and take* works much better than *take and give*. Of course, someone has to *take* (receive), or else the whole thing breaks down. But imagine a marriage where each partner is fighting for the privilege of giving first. Someone still has to submit—and receive—but that kind of fight (fighting for the other person, really) leads to laughter, lovemaking and a lifetime of affection.

In Ephesians 5, the Bible talks about mutual submission—give and take—as God's model for marriage. To the original readers of Ephesians, this was extremely countercultural and eons before its time, as the mores of that day dictated that husbands literally owned their wives. It's still galaxies ahead of us, as we scramble to "look out for number one" and "make sure I get mine" in our me-centered culture.

Philippians 2:3 encourages us to consider the other person more important than ourselves. It doesn't say the other person *is* more important. But it urges us to develop an attitude like Jesus', which puts the other in a place of priority. This means, quite literally, submitting my opinion, my hopes, my dreams, and my preferences into a secondary slot beneath and behind those of my spouse.

STOP, TALK AND LISTEN

1. Are you more prone to take first or give first? Why?
2. Some relationships function with one person doing the greater part of the giving. How would it make you feel to be that person?
3. The word *submit* sends some people running for the hills. What does it mean to you?
4. Are you willing to consider the other person more important than yourself? Why or why not?

When Wrong Is Oh So Right

So what if my spouse is wrong? What if I'm right? What if doing it the other way makes no sense to me? Why should I be the one to submit?

Because showing respect is so much more important than being right on any particular issue. Getting one's way is like winning a battle. Honoring one's spouse is like winning the whole war. Giving way is not only wise; it is strong and generous and forward thinking.

compromise

The challenge, of course, is never saying or implying "I told you so" if my spouse's approach turns out to be costly. I shared in this decision by choosing to submit and honor that approach. We arrived at our course of action together and we will manage the fallout together.

And, conversely, when she's so completely right, Wow! It's a good thing I honored her view.

I've discovered that my wife is remarkably intuitive. When I've blown through her point of view, refusing to honor or submit to it, it has been to my utter folly.

Mostly, she seems eager to submit to me, also. Not because I ask for it. If I have to ask for submission I must have blown her trust a long time ago. She's eager to respect my views because she knows that her views have a hearing and are not dismissed or overridden. She also submits readily because she owns this Christlike value of strong servanthood, hearty submission and mutual respect.

STOP, TALK AND LISTEN

1. Think about a time when you knew you were right and wouldn't submit. How did things go?
2. Think about a time when you each argued for the other's view. How did that go?
3. Are there issues that are too important to give in and relinquish your opinion? Consider potential examples.

What About Male Headship?

Male leadership is obviously a biblical mandate. Ephesians 5:22 tells the woman to submit to the man as if he were Jesus. "For the husband is the head of the wife as Christ is the head of the church" (verse 23). In Paul's male-dominant culture, the male reader said a hearty "amen" and the female said, "Yeah, yeah, we know."

Then comes the next line. "Husbands, love your wives, just as Christ loved the church and gave himself up for her" (verse 25). Not by being domineering. Not by demanding his own way. Jesus loved his bride, the church, by meeting us where we live; walking in our flesh, teaching, modeling, giving, serving, proving what the love of God looks like. He quite literally laid down his life for us! That's the image intended here. Total servant leadership.

That's male headship according to Scripture. Living the Christ life.

But doesn't the buck stop with me? Okay, there is a sense of accountability in Christian Scripture that a man carries for the well-being of his bride and the family. But this responsibility is only wielded well when it's done as service—motivated by a will to give and empowered by a heart of kindness. Power trips and ego-based headship have absolutely nothing to do with Jesus, Christianity or God's intention for marriage.

Are there moments for tough love? Of course. If someone is truly doing harm, confrontation becomes necessary. Jesus taught this and modeled it. But the stories of Jesus' confrontation are few and far between, compared to example after example of his gentle guidance and healing intervention.

In short, male headship is all about being the head servant of the household. I have never met a woman who resented that kind of leadership in the home, except in cases where she was convicted by it and chose shame and anger instead of thankful participation.

STOP, TALK AND LISTEN

1. How do you feel about male headship in the family?
2. How did your parents handle authority and decision making?
3. Have you seen a couple do male headship well? What does it look like?

More About Role-Playing

Of course, most decision making lays down gently according to talents, giftedness and natural roles. My wife is better at detailed budgeting and I'm better at big-picture investing. So she does microfinance and I do the macro. My wife loves to cook and I find dishwashing relaxing. While the roles occasionally flip-flop, and sometimes my evening meetings leave her doing both tasks, the system works pretty well.

Trouble comes when the weight of the work is unevenly proportioned. If one person has all the gross jobs, or has to do all the heavy lifting, that spouse can start feeling ill-used and even mistreated.

In the past, roles laid down easier, with cleaner lines. Husbands worked outside the home and wives did the equivalent of a full-time job making the household function. Assuming that both worked heartily, and shared parenting tasks, the distribution worked for many (not all, of course).

Today, with women in every avenue of work outside the home, it's harder to navigate role distribution. In some homes, the wife works a paying job all day and then continues to work all night at home, while the husband comes home and kicks back. To some degree, studies show that women have more durability and tenacity for working all day, while men tend to work in great blasts of energy and then suffer real exhaustion. Even our core body types contribute to this explanation.

Still, there's something patently unfair about that arrangement. Sometimes a man needs to save some of his better energies for home, so that he can make significant contributions. And sometimes a woman needs to relax some expectations. Working outside of the home comes with costs and benefits. One benefit might be the extra income to pay someone else to do some things around the home (and even make a living at it) rather than demanding that either or both partners do the equivalent of two jobs.

In other words, men and women, don't be a martyr and don't find yourself in the awful position of being a nag. Spend time talking about equitable, functional role distribution, and then recalibrate if something isn't working.

STOP, TALK AND LISTEN

1. What will your role distribution look like? Who will do what?
2. Can you imagine one of you feeling like a martyr? Which one and why? How can you head this off?
3. If you are both working outside the home, then the care of the home lands on the both of you. Are you sure this is what you want? How about when kids arrive?

Drafting on Each Other

Life and marriage have taught me that God uses my wife as a leader in our relationship when I'm tired or weak or depressed or misguided. And God has used me in the same way for her.

Years ago, I experienced a season of depression. It took me by surprise. It took weeks, maybe months, for me to even admit that I was in depression's clutches. When I finally acknowledged my plight, Sue simply said, "What do you feel like you need?" My answer spilled out. "I feel like I need to sleep in. I need to swim with our daughter every day. I need to play golf once a week. Sorry. It sounds so selfish."

compromise

Sue cleared space for weekly tee times and gave total emotional support to this indulgence. She called my supervisor to tell him that I'd be coming in late for a season. She laid my swimsuit on the bed and prepared our daughter for a swim almost every evening. She accepted wholesale leadership of our home for nine months, while I coursed through the grief and frustrations that led to depression. And when it was over, she never made me feel beholden to her.

Some of our most jarring conflicts have come when we were both weary or wounded, and wished (consciously or not) that the other had the strength to step up.

That highlights the need for community, church, friends, family, counselors, pastors—anyone and everyone who can come alongside us when neither is in a healthy season or a strong state of mind.

STOP, TALK AND LISTEN

1. Are there times when you really *love* to be led?
2. Do you remember a time when you had to completely rely on others to get you through?
3. Have you had a time when you were both so weary that neither was in a position to guide you through?

Simply Ask and Tell

"This is what I feel." "That is what I am hoping for." "These are my dreams. Can you help me realize them?"

If all of that sounds corny, then we're just not paying attention.

Years ago, I struggled with the notion of having to ask my wife's permission to play golf. And she *hated* playing the parent. If I asked, and she said "no," I resented her answer and she felt guilty and frustrated about being put in that position.

Finally, we learned a language. "Here are my hopes for golf. My goal is to play once every two weeks. Occasionally more, occasionally less. But I want to do this in a way that doesn't stress the household or put undue pressure on you to 'permit' me to play." So, together, we talked about how this could work. Sue invested interest and really participated in my dream.

I try *never* to ask my wife's permission for anything. It puts her in an unfair position. Instead, I ask the question, "How would this or that affect the flow of your day, or the family?" Then I make the call with whatever information she gives me. Of course, sometimes she says, "That just wouldn't work." But I haven't set her up to be the spoiler. If it doesn't work for her, it doesn't work for me.

And besides, have you ever played a round of golf (or any other game or hobby) knowing full well that you're in the wrong place? It's actually a miserable experience.

STOP, TALK AND LISTEN

1. Do you find yourself asking or giving permission?
2. Do you ever feel mothered or fathered by the other?
3. Is it okay to communicate your hopes and solicit partnership without asking permission?

Are Patriarchies or Matriarchies Always Wrong?

In some cases, with some blends of personalities, patriarchies and matriarchies actually work. Like with benevolent monarchies, strong and kind leadership from one spouse can mean streamlined decision making and a pretty functional home.

If.

If the other partner truly doesn't mind handing off most decisions, and actually appreciates freedom from the burden

compromise

of leading. There are personality types—some quite phlegmatic (going with the flow) and others very sanguine (play, play, play)—who really don't mind being led by a spouse.

And if.

If the benevolent dictator really doesn't mind carrying the burden of decision making. Some people are simply born to lead, and making decisions is what they do all day every day. They thrive on it, and it gives them energy.

I could never be happy doing this. I love empowering others and eliciting shared ownership of decisions. I wouldn't want to be led all the time and I absolutely hate dictating—even though most people who know me well would call me a natural leader.

But some people are happy in these lopsided relationships and I'm tired of judging this approach as altogether bad. It's not my ideal because most people couldn't abide it; but some can.

STOP, TALK AND LISTEN

1. Could you tolerate—even enjoy—a benevolent monarchy? Why or why not?
2. What would you do if authority tilted toward you? How would you ask for more balance?
3. What would you do if authority tilted away from you? How would you ask for more balance?

"What Ifs" and "What Abouts"

What if I'm in a relationship that feels lopsided, and I don't like being domineered?

It's time for some honesty. "I can endure a relationship that discounts viewpoints and concerns, but I'm not sure I can enjoy one. Is there a way we can share decision making more? I would feel more respect and camaraderie." Do you see the "I" language?

By the way, be sure to look in the mirror. Is there a way in which you naturally disrespect yourself and virtually invite the domination of another? Find a friend and dig away at this possibility.

What if I'm doing all the giving and my spouse is doing all the taking?

Again, some honesty is in order: "I can probably endure a relationship where it feels like I'm doing most of the giving, but I'm not sure I can enjoy one. Is there a way in which we can be more mutual in sharing tasks, building a partnership and making things happen together?"

By the way, time to look in the mirror. Many people who "do all the work" chase away potential shareholders by being finicky, ornery and otherwise miserable to work with. If your spouse has to do something a certain way in order to pass inspection, you can imagine that your spouse will lose interest, and even resent the task.

Then again, if you ask well: "Here are my hopes and dreams. Do you see any way that we could partner to help these things happen?" Chances are you'll have a hearty investor.

compromise

My life is one big compromise. I laid down all of my dreams when I got married.

Find a third party to talk to. First, communicate these losses to this friend or counselor. Then, with your friend's help, decide which dreams are worthy of communicating to your spouse.

Some *aren't* worthy. They simply represent the truth that all of us kiss away some benefits of being single when we kiss at the altar.

Some *are* worthy. These failed hopes need to be flushed out and either grieved (because they'll never actually come true) or reawakened (because they still can come true.) Don't stew, grouse and poison your marriage with resentment.

What about the bedroom? Who leads there?

By God's grace he created us to enjoy making our partners "turned on." In most cases, it's as arousing, or more, to see the *other* enjoy. So give and take. Take turns leading. If you refuse to receive, the other can't give. If you refuse to give, the other can't receive, and you're robbing yourself of life's greatest pleasure. In this regard, it is truly more blessed to give than to receive.

If you never lead, the other will doubt your interest. If you never let the other lead, you're withholding the pleasure of servanthood from your spouse.

All this to say, *go for it!* Let the bedroom be a frequent laboratory for fleshing out the principles of God's design. Reciprocity!

And give a lot of grace. It's not like the movies.

love

It's more than merely a feeling—
and I feel a lot!
This is a matter of the will.
I will never stop loving you.

You would think that love would be the first *building block* to surface as premarried couples make their lists. Actually, it usually goes unsaid until one person says, "Oh, and love, of course." And both laugh at having missed the simple and obvious.

Obvious, yes.

Simple, no.

We say we love baseball and we love hamburgers. We say we love our parents and we love our friends. We say we love our favorite music groups and we love God. Can one word—love—really cover the scope of all those emotions and affections?

And what do we mean when we tell our *lovers,* "I love you"? Are we talking about romantic love? Familial love? Friendship love? Loyalty love? Sacrificial love? French fry love?

Fortunately, the Bible is written in a language—Greek—that offers more clarity than English in regard to love.

STOP, TALK AND LISTEN

1. Where was love on your list? Did it pop to mind quickly or later as the "Oh, yeah?"
2. How would you each define love?

Eros Is Pretty Great

We get our word "erotic" from the Greek word *eros*. *Eros* means sexual and romantic love. It's one of our favorite loves; the stuff that dreams and fairy tales are made of.

But here's the problem. In almost every marriage (maybe *every* marriage) *eros* ebbs and flows, wanes and surges. When romance is running high, marriage is hot. When the sparks aren't flying, hot isn't the word.

Building a marriage on *eros* is like building a dock on a tidal plain. When the tide is in, we float blissfully on a sea of emotion. But when the tide is out, marriage can be hard and dry. We need more than *eros* to build on.

Sexual, romantic love often brings us together. Attractions that flow beyond all reason draw us together. But those pulsing emotions can't be trusted without testing and measuring a relationship with other kinds of love.

Sometimes couples marry because the "sex is hot." I believe them. It is hot . . . today! But what about tomorrow? Some couples marry because they are sexually addicted to each other and literally are unable to pull away even though the relationship is not based on better kinds of love. Those are so often miserable marriages.

Too often, I'll meet couples who give up on marriage. One tired rationale for divorce goes like this: "We fell out of love." Of course, I don't believe they "fell out" any more than I believe they "fell in." What they mean is that their *eros* has run dry. What they may not know is that most, if not all, couples face the same reality in seasons.

So why marry if the fun goes away? Well, fortunately, it doesn't have to go away forever. Better yet, there are deeper and better loves that provide a firmer foundation than *eros*. *Eros* is great! But it's the icing on the cake. It draws the eye. It adds a certain sweetness and flavor. But the real cake is something else. Something better.

STOP, TALK AND LISTEN

1. Do you ever wonder if you've built too much of your relationship on *eros*?
2. Do you think you are physically addicted to the physical touch or sexual exchanges you've already experienced?
3. Can you endure a marriage in which sex is affected by a physical or emotional problem? Are other loves strong enough to compensate?

What About *Philos*?

Most people know that Philadelphia is "the City of Brotherly Love." Few know why.

Phila comes from *philos,* which in Greek means "brotherly love." *Philos* is that affection and loyalty that we feel for a true brother or a heartfelt friend. And what a crucial love this is. Blood, experience, laughter, war, ball games, coffee chats—all of these things tie us to one another in ways that really matter.

But here's a challenge: we can distance ourselves from siblings and walk away from friendships whenever those relationships are hurtful or unsatisfying. There is no cultural or biblical teaching against simply kissing our *philos* relationships goodbye. Yes, the Bible teaches forgiveness and Jesus is all about reconciliation. But no one, not even Jesus, suggests that we *must* stay with a friend or family member with whom we're "just not getting along."

Except with our spouses. Marriage is a lifetime commitment to stay together—and even to stay close—until we die. Many marriages have plenty of *philos* to fuel them. Throw in some occasional *eros* and shouldn't that be enough?

Well, it is. Except when it isn't.

Conflicts, tragedies, funks and misunderstandings of every kind can make *philos* elusive. If marriage is built primarily on *philos,* troubles might be too much to endure.

STOP, TALK AND LISTEN

1. How is your *philos* factor? Are you good friends and companions, *eros* aside?
2. Did you watch *philos* in your parents? What lessons have you learned from their successes and failures in friendship?

Agapé, the Best Foundation

Agapé is loyal love. *Agapé* is committed love. *Agapé* is sacrificial love. *Agapé* is stubborn love. *Agapé* is active, self-giving love. It's a love that says, "I love you forever, even when I don't feel like loving you." It's love that keeps showing up and doing the right thing even when emotions are dry and friendship is strained.

Agapé is what some call "unconditional love." You hurt me? I love you back. Life tries to separate us? I won't go away. You change and I change but this won't change—I love you today and I will love you tomorrow. Nothing will stop me from loving you because I won't let it happen. I may not be perfect and I might disappoint in a hundred different ways. But you can count on this: I love you.

Agapé is servant love. It means, "I will give and serve and listen and care and provide even if there is no reciprocity. In sickness and in health, for richer or poorer, my love for you is a matter of the *will* and not merely emotion.

It's a Supernatural Thing

So where does this love come from? Isn't the human story stained by our inability to muster up this extreme and generous love?

It's astonishing how some people are capable of extraordinary measures of *agapé*. I've seen spouses of disabled or mentally impaired loved ones just *gut it out.* They keep giving and loving and caring, even when the spouse is unable or unwilling to give in return. These lovers are walking miracles and true heroes on this planet.

Occasionally, I've met people like that who seem preconditioned by nature or upbringing to behave in such loyal ways—independent from an active faith in God.

Usually when I meet people like this I find out that God is a source of authority, inspiration and strength. These generous lovers feel compelled by God's value system regarding the covenantal nature of marriage. They feel reliant on the companionship of God and God's church to compensate for the lost love of a difficult spouse. And they feel truly helped by prayer, Scripture, the Holy Spirit and the hope of heaven. They keep coming and loving and staying and serving, because that is what a life under the influence of God is bound to do.

I'm saying that strong Christians (not merely cultural Christians or lip-service Christians) do *agapé* better. And I challenge you to prove otherwise!

STOP, TALK AND LISTEN

1. Do you rely on God to give you supernatural help in loving your partner?
2. Do you have access to God and God's teachings in a way that resources you for your marriage?
3. Do either of you have a natural predisposition for this kind of love, or do you know someone like this?

So How Do I Get Some of That?

Pray. Ask God to enter into your heart. Invite Jesus to forgive you and save you from a self-serving way of life. Commit to his teachings. Study his words. Follow his example. Ask for God's Spirit to fill you and change you and inspire you and comfort you in times when life gets hard. Make a vow to love and cherish Christ, just as you make a vow to love your spouse, "for better or worse" as long as you live. In other words, be a Christian, which is a disciple or apprentice of Jesus Christ. And God will prove himself. If you are genuine and a true seeker, God will provide the will and the way.

STOP, TALK AND LISTEN

1. Are you a Christian? Tell your partner the level of your spiritual interest and the story of your faith journey. If you've already done this, do it again!

How Do I Know?

God is an inexhaustible source of this *agapé* love. The most famous verse in the Bible says that "God so *agapéd* the world that he gave his one and only Son."[13] Jesus taught that there is no greater commandment than to *agapé* God with our whole beings and to *agapé* our neighbors as we *agapé* ourselves.[14]

---

13 John 3:16.
14 Matthew 22:37-39.

He said that the essence of *agapé* is to lay down our lives and he proved his own *agapé* by doing exactly that.[15]

Paul teaches husbands to *agapé* their wives and he teaches husbands and wives to "submit to one another out of reverence for Christ,"[16] which is a fundamental part of *agapé*—self-surrender and servanthood.

Here is the nutshell version of Christianity: *agapé* God, one another, even your enemies, and certainly love yourself in healthy, generous ways.

Here is the nutshell version of marriage: *agapé* each other. Marriage is supposed to be a model and a testing ground for this countercultural manner of living.

STOP, TALK AND LISTEN

1. Does all of this *agapé* talk scare you? If so, why? Afraid you can't do it? Afraid your spouse can't?
2. Do you know how much God loves you?
3. Since secure people tend to love more and better, are you a secure person in the love of God and others? If not, what now?

"What Ifs" and "What Abouts"

What if my love really does run dry?

First, remember that feelings are more or less acute in various seasons of our lives. No matter how difficult, there are dull seasons in every relationship. Beyond that very ordinary reality, there are things that can be done. Search your heart to see if

15 John 10:11; 15:13.
16 Ephesians 5:21.

you're holding onto wrongs suffered that you need to let go of and forgive. Alter your routine and breathe some fresh air into the relationship. Go new places. Plan some date nights. Get away for a weekend. Let the relationship benefit from renewed focus. Turn up the dial sexually. Pray, pray, pray for a heart that is warmed toward your partner. And really, call a counselor whenever it seems helpful.

I realize now that so much of our relationship has been built on eros. *But I can't pull out of the marriage now. What do I do?*

If you aren't married, I suggest a sexual fast. Some of us do this with food to free ourselves from the grip of our appetites, in order to gain new spiritual insight. You can do the same with sex. Of course, your partner needs to know what you're doing. Invite him/her in. Whether you've been *fully* active sexually or not, physical dependence or addiction can set in. So spend this time (weeks?) without the bonding agents of physical caress and see what happens to your affections. If you feel greater distance, this will indicate a problem. If all you feel is sexual pull, this also indicates a problem. But if the relationship flourishes, you may have a different answer—other critical *building blocks* are at play in securing a strong relationship. If you're not married, wait for your wedding night, which will allow you to keep building on the other *blocks.* When you are married, use all the blocks—don't revert back to relying on *eros.* Just enjoy it!

Agapé *love sounds like a reach for me. I'm pretty conditional in the way I love.*

Be honest with your partner and go together into a journey of faith. Go to church—a good one that tells the Christian story in transformative ways. Try praying together, even if it feels clunky at first. Practice loving *well,* even when you're frustrated with your partner. Give. Forgive. Serve. Keep a humble spirit. See what happens.

CHAPTER 6

loyalty

We are FOR each other.
Our words, our actions;
when we're together or apart;
we are a team.

When some premarriage couples land on the word *loyalty,* one person says the word with a lilt in the voice that seems to say, "Please don't leave me out here alone. I'm intending to be loyal. Will you, too?" It's almost a moan of vulnerability, an appeal born out of some past hurt. Perhaps he's suffered the disloyalty of a parent who disrupted family unity, or she's suffered past relationships in which her own loyalty wasn't matched by a partner.

In other cases, there's a tone of confidence and conviction to this declaration. "We believe in loyalty. We will be loyal."

In the first case, the obvious vulnerability leads to a significant discussion. "Why do I hear pain in your voice? Is there something your partner needs to know in order to offer a degree of loyalty that fosters security and confidence?"

In the second case, that bold voice of conviction begs the question, "Why do couples who declare their loyalty with every strong assurance *still* fall into behaviors and alliances that become disloyal? Are there ways to prevent loyalty leakage and to live out higher ideals?"

STOP, TALK AND LISTEN

1. Have you been burned by disloyalty in a relationship? Do some storytelling.
2. Are you confident in your capacity for loyalty? Why?

What Is Loyalty?

The topic of loyalty intersects with our previous study of trust. Loyalty breeds trust. Loyalty secures trust. What, then, does it mean to be loyal, and why is it so important?

Couples tend to define loyalty as the emotional covenant that says, "There are aspects of relationship that I reserve solely for you. You are the only one to whom I bare my body and soul. There is something intimate about what we share that is stronger, closer, more long lasting and, ultimately, more important than any other human tie."

When that covenant is broken by another usurping relationship, the offended partner will feel that the other has been disloyal. When one partner puts another relationship in a higher place of priority and energy, the offended partner will be just that—offended.

STOP, TALK AND LISTEN

1. Are you ready for this kind of loyalty—above all other human relationships?
2. Is there already a relationship or activity in either life that tends to steal top honors? A sport? A job? A best friend? A parent? What will you do about it?

unshakable

74

Types of Disloyalty

Most notoriously, loyalty is broken by sexual wanderings. Affairs are the more aggressive examples, while flirtations and obsessions (like pornography) will also cause fractures and pains; especially if these behaviors are secretive.

But there are other relational areas where loyalty is put to the test. For example, most of us would like to know that our spouses speak well of us in our absence.

In our first church, several women organized a discussion and support group using the book *Creative Counterpart* by Linda Dillow as the curriculum, which by all reports is a very useful book.[17] After a few weeks, husbands began to show up at my door and in my ear.

"This *Creative Counterpart* meeting has turned into a big gabfest."

"I feel like our dirty laundry is getting hung up all over the church."

"All they do at those meetings is complain about their husbands."

"I don't feel safe anymore."

My own wife attended a meeting or two and reported that the men's fears were completely warranted. Secrets were being revealed; flaws laid open for lamentation and critique; stories told. All in all, it was a well-intentioned skewering of the husbands. A few ground rules and encouragements brought this worthy effort into a more loyal and respectful pattern.

But what I heard from the men was this: "She's being disloyal. I don't spew her garbage all over town."

And men usually don't—at least, not in detail. In generalities, men can often disparage their wives with sweeping labels and impressions. "The old *ball-and-chain* won't let me go out tonight." Or, "The *boss* says I have to babysit." Or, "It's the time of the month when I have to hide all sharp and heavy objects

---

17 Linda Dillow, *Creative Counterpart: Becoming the Woman, Wife and Mother You Have Longed to Be* (Nashville: Thomas Nelson), 2003.

in the home." While quips like these can alleviate stress among friends, just as detailed lamentation does for women, talk like that can also be very disloyal.

"I thought you were *for* me," she says. "But now I know that I'm a witch and a burden—a disappointing caricature."

STOP, TALK AND LISTEN

1. Have you experienced this or not? Do both of you feel emotionally safe when your partner is with others?
2. Do you feel honored by the way your partner speaks about you?

Who Do I Talk To?

Everyone, of course, needs to blow off steam to a trusted friend every once in a while. Most of us are smart to have a confidante other than our spouses; someone with whom we can vent and filter. My suggestion is simply this: make sure that person is preapproved with your spouse.

Your partner needs confidence in knowing that private information won't be spilled all over town. And he or she doesn't need an antagonist who is driving a wedge between you and your partner, which is what some friends do. Almost without exception, confide in someone of the same gender. I say almost. Sometimes age disparity can make someone of the opposite gender a safe confidante. Or there might be other reasons why this person of the other gender is totally safe. But as a whole, a same-gender friend works best.

STOP, TALK AND LISTEN

1. Who do you each really trust with personal information?
2. Do you both trust the person that the other trusts?

Why So Vigilant?

First, a breach in loyalty causes a breach in trust; and a loss of trust means a loss of peace and confidence. All of this harms intimacy. It even affects people's capacity to function during a day. Because my wife is loyal to me, I can work, play, sleep and pray without the disruptive fears and jealousies that rob contentment and fog my life focus. Were I not able to trust her, my life would be shackled with doubt and uncertainty.

But there's more. As a parent, I want to teach my children how to be loyal to others in relationships—especially marital—even when circumstances are difficult. As children watch us, they do *what we do* more than they do *what we say*. I know that this book is about marriage and not about parenting, but our marriages affect others. People around us—mostly our children—draw courage and perspective from our ability to stay loyal to vows and covenants that we've made before God and witnesses. In the bigger picture, the whole fabric of society tears apart when these fundamental loyalties are too easily broken.

STOP, TALK AND LISTEN

1. What did you watch your parents do? Were they loyal?
2. What are your takeaways from watching your parents? Any particular strengths or vulnerabilities?

Where Do We Draw the Line?

So where is the line with secondary relationships, confidential conversations and even harmless flirtations?

The line might be set differently for every couple; and it may be different in various seasons of life for each couple. For example, one young marriage might be threatened by little flirtations with friends of the opposite gender, since loyalty and trust haven't been able to set like concrete. Years later, the same level

loyalty

of flirtation could be a source of laughter and mutual affection. "Flirt with him all you want, but I know you're mine!"

Another marriage might be affected in the opposite way. Early on, confidence could be high in one another. Later, with changing bodies and sagging self-confidence, a previously harmless flirtation could be a critical body blow to the marriage.

Talk. Communicate. Understand the seasons of life and the unique story of your partner.

Men frequently flirt with my wife. She's outwardly attractive. She's a warm person. She's smart and rapier-quick with comebacks. She enjoys verbal sparring, born out of close relationships with her father and brothers. Men light up around her. Almost always, this is fine with me. The interest of other men feels like a compliment to us both—until. Sometimes someone pushes it too far and the guy bugs me. This little dance is complex. But over the years, we're learning to read the signals of when these interactions are *not* fun. And, as I've said before, trusting my wife gives me freedom to live in undistracted ways.

As a pastor, I interact with many women. Often, because of my idealism and pastoral manner, I represent parts and pieces of what women *wish* they saw in their husbands. I listen. I "get" things that other guys seem to miss. Usually, when my wife sees a few wistful glances or come-on-ish behaviors, she isn't bothered—until. Over the years, we've navigated this together. We learn to say, "It bothers me when ..." or "I feel threatened by this person because...." And we practice steering clear and avoiding situations that could incite fear or jealousy in the other.

My wife knows when *not* to let someone into the house; and she tells me quickly about the incidents and encounters that reveal the predatory and opportunistic nature of some men. And I'm learning to anticipate the kinds of interactions that will make my wife grind her teeth or worry.

1. Are there moments when jealousy affects either of you? Who or what triggers this?
2. When you are apart, do you both feel confidence and peace about the whereabouts and activities of your partner?

What Do Your Vows Mean?

There's still more. Loyalty means staying together through hard and dark seasons. Life brings strains of every kind. People change. Depression or physical illness can set in. Physical and emotional cycles play out their parts. Loyalty says, "I'm not going anywhere. The things said at the altar are like words etched in stone: "For better or worse; for richer or poorer; in sickness and in health, 'til death do us part." Those words meant something when I said them, and they mean far more to me today.

For some people, those words are ceremonial more than actual. "For better or worse (unless things get really bad!); for richer or poorer (but I'm not going to be destitute!); in sickness and in health (as long as you don't become a bummer to live with!), 'til death do us part (or until I fall out of love!)."

You have the seasons of dating and engagement to smoke out the truth about yourself and your prospective spouse. If you don't see real, robust loyalty, please, *don't marry!* Just don't go through with it.

But if you do go through with it, then *stay with it.* Let loyalty lead you to the deepest and best human relationship imaginable. Be loyal to the dream of *being* together, not just staying together. Keep showing up. Keep listening and learning. Keep forgiving. And never, never stop working on this critical friendship.

Loyalty will pay off. Whatever happens and however hard it is, God rewards covenant loyalty with spiritual riches that transcend mere marital bliss.

loyalty

"What Ifs" and "What Abouts"

What if my partner keeps saying she'll be loyal but the secret-telling never stops?

Keep encouraging her to choose friends and confidantes who can handle personal information well. And make sure you are practicing good listening skills so that she doesn't have to go to others for a sympathetic ear.

What if my partner can't cut the apron strings from his mom? She's driving me crazy! I didn't know I was marrying her, too.

You aren't. And he needs to make his loyalty clear; you must be able to trust that his loyalty is first and foremost to you, and he needs to make sure that Mom knows this, too. Some moms try to wedge into relationships because they fear they are losing their beloved sons to another woman. So here's the truth—they are! The sooner Mom knows and accepts this, the better for everyone. Even in cases of widowhood, she has to realize that her son can no longer be her primary source of help and intimacy. Men, grow up and love your moms well—as the number two woman in your lives. And if push comes to shove, pick your side of the skirmish right now—and I don't mean Mom's side!

My fiancé is very attractive. I'm constantly fending off flirtatious people. It's bugging me!

Realize that the attractive features are what attracted you as well. Don't ask your partner to change. Still, you can develop a language together; even a code for public places. These cues can communicate when you want him/her all to yourself. And if there is a type of person who makes you feel unsafe, you can communicate this honestly so that your partner can practice keeping some distance from those types.

Be encouraged. Loyalty over time breeds trust. A day might come when you're actually flattered by knowing that other people find your partner attractive. Let that truth fuel your thanksgiving and affection.

My fiancé wants to change our vows. They're beautiful words, but not nearly as binding. What do I say?

Tell the truth about how you feel. Make sure that there are profoundly binding aspects to your covenant. If your partner doesn't like it, beware. Sorry to make you queasy, but if your partner is afraid of commitment, he/she might not be very good at it.

CHAPTER 7

laughter

Sure, the family that prays together stays together.
But so does the family that plays together
and revels in the humor of life.

My mind drifts back to one season of illness when my wife suffered the trauma of breast cancer. I shudder at the thought of all she had to endure and the fears that threatened our family.

Then the laughter rolls in.

Laughter?

Yes. My wife battled cancer with a macabre sense of humor that defied the dark edge of depression. On top of that, we purchased every season of our favorite television sitcom, and then watched and howled until the funniest dialogues on that show were etched into our family vocabulary.

Laughter saved us.

Of course, God saved us. And doctors and treatments. But I remember laughter's medicine most and best.

I'm not as funny as my wife. I can be silly and quippy and occasionally something very dry and smart will come out of me. Sue, on the other hand, has a rare comedic gift that usually pops out at home and in trusted social settings.

In sickness or in health, I want to be fun to live with. That's one reason my wife married me—to have fun. Now's not the time to pull a bait-and-switch. How common it is to hear women say, "He was fun when we were dating. Now he's a couch potato. Where's the guy who wooed me and won me?"

Conversations with men who have affairs, usually fifteen to twenty-five years into marriage, have revealed a lot about this aspect of marriage. I had always assumed that men wanted sex with younger women because of their tight bodies and smooth shining skin. Instead, many men say, "She was fun. Somewhere along the way, my wife quit being fun. Don't you find that younger women are just more fun?"

"Okay, but that doesn't justify a thing!" I judge instantly. And it doesn't. But as I hear the stories, I hear the pain of relationships that lose their laughter, spontaneity and playfulness. While I always urge men (and women) back into marriage, I'm not too arrogant to sympathize. It is sad when the fun fizzles. And sad people often make bad choices.

STOP, TALK AND LISTEN

1. Do you have fun together? Share examples of the kinds of fun and laughter that need to continue no matter what.
2. During dating and engagement, you mostly see the best in each other. Marriage can bring out the worst. Why?

Where Did the Laughter Go?

Life does this to us, and it doesn't only happen to women or men. The burdens of job, family and aging can make laughter elusive. Heaviness can set in, especially when forgiveness is withheld by either or both parties.

Without forgiveness, kiss laughter good-bye. Keep a long list of wrongs suffered and you will rob your marriage of laughter. Imagine the effect of replacing episodes of laughter with fault finding and grudge nursing. Such an attitude is devastating to a marriage.

We'll deal with forgiveness in another chapter. But for now, please remember that laughter needs a runway that's free from the debris of unforgiven slights.

STOP, TALK AND LISTEN

1. Can you identify heavy things that tend to steal your laughter?

Where Does Laughter Come From?

What's true in television sitcoms is mostly true in our lives. Laughter comes from little nothings—the things that happen *to* us and *in* us and *around* us. Almost everything is fair game. Practice laughing at life. Keep laughing with each other. Go ahead and tease, poke, rib and flirt. Hold on to some childlikeness in the same way you try to hold on to your athleticism and youthful beauty. Those things will go away eventually, but childlikeness can actually grow back again!

Keep delighting in little things—the best bite from a delicious dinner; the sunset over a shadowy hill; the quirky things that make people unique; the way people look like their dogs; the spilled milk and burned rice; the hilarity of sex—trying to be all cool but....

Instead of becoming rigid and dark and moody and heavy, be inflexible only on this—"I will not stop laughing!"

Go on dates. Hold hands. Pick and follow a favorite comedian. Peek around the corner and watch the children's antics. Choose friends that make you laugh, or bring out your lighter side. Play stupid practical jokes.

laughter

STOP, TALK AND LISTEN

1. What TV show, old or new, really makes you laugh out loud? Why?
2. Is there a friend, or a couple, with whom laughter comes easily? Do you spend time with them?

When Things Get Tough

Believe me; I'm not saying that this is always easy. As I mentioned earlier, I've had at least one season of honest-to-goodness depression. Laughing didn't come freely and I relied on my wife for most of the levity in the home. But I also sought help and followed a careful program toward wellness. My wife was the best solution. She was amazing.

Even healthy seasons can be heavy. In healthy seasons, this is the biggest issue—don't burn all of your best energy during the day. Don't expend the good energy at work so that all you bring home is a tired shell of yourself. Don't even expend all of your best self on the children. Save energy and find energy for each other.

Too many people—especially men—have affairs at work *with* work. In other words, vocation becomes a replacement spouse. People go to great lengths to justify their ambitions for status or wealth, often claiming that they are "doing it for their families." If they were to honestly ask, "What's best for my family?" the answer would not come back, "Spend more time and your best energy at work."

Even in ministry, where the work is often weighted by eternal significance and human crises, the temptation is always there to pour myself out until I have nothing left for my wife and children. Sometimes, I can dig deep and do it all for church and family, but that's not sustainable. I usually have to pace myself and preserve precious energy for the precious people at home.

One trick I've learned is to stop for coffee on the way home (not for alcohol, which is a depressant). Or else, I take a ten-minute joyride on the way home, simply to allow my batteries to recharge and to flush out the stresses of the day. I want to be able to alleviate the pressure of the home when I walk in, rather than dwelling on the stress of my day.

As for the children, don't dump all of your best energy on them. I love kids, but no child benefits from the faulty notion that he or she is the center of our universe. The health of spiritual and marital relationships creates a home culture of wholeness and nurture where children thrive. Any parent who puts the children ahead of the marriage and even ahead of personal health and wholeness is displacing affection and disordering priorities. Being the center of the universe is a heavy burden for a child; when we rely on children to make us feel happy or fulfilled, we do them a disservice.

So get healthy and stay healthy. Yes, "the family that prays together stays together." But so does the family that plays together. Play well. Play hard. Play fair. And laugh.

STOP, TALK AND LISTEN

1. Can you foresee the heaviness of work or family stealing away laughter from your relationship?
2. Have you learned some tricks or techniques to help you decompress and then reengage after a hard day?

It Starts with Me

A healthy relationship starts with good self-care. Self-love is often the forgotten love. Staying healthy allows us to bring mostly health to our relationships. There's a fine line between

laughter

self-indulgence and self-care, but experiment with where that line is. People who love themselves love others more effectively. So exercise, play and allow a strong devotional life to feed your soul. Have enough hobbies to recreate—literally re-create. And come to your marriage as a healthy contributor.

Except when you can't. Then take your pain and brokenness and heaviness to God—and, yes, also to your spouse. Nurse each other. Help each other. Marriage is rarely 50-50. It usually requires one to give a bit more depending on the season.

I don't want to be fatalistic about the trials you will face together. However, even Jesus promises, "In the world you will have trouble."[18] He has overcome the world, and we can also overcome our problems and issues. One of the tools for overcoming with God's help is laughter. Feed and sustain this good habit and the tough seasons ahead may not be *as* tough.

"What Ifs" and "What Abouts"

What if he gets lost in his work? I saw my dad do it and it seems like a guy thing.

Support his work and encourage him to be a champion in whatever he does. But don't stop talking together about how to bring order and balance to your life. Don't nag, but make sure he knows how much you love to have him home with you—and not just to rescue you from the kids or from your loneliness. Build a good life for yourself, and urge him to come home to spend quality time with a whole person.

18 John 16:33.

By the way, women can get caught up in work, too. For some reason, most women are able to dig deeper and keep giving even after a hard day at work. Some researchers suggest that the female body and psyche are geared for enduring, long-term exertions, while men are geared for rocket-launch exertions followed by the need for considerable refueling.

That can be really frustrating! He seems to "veg out" more than I thought he would. He's boring!

This is a common report. Yes, most men head straight for the remote control when they need downtime. Negotiate this. Allow for some recovery time in the evening; but men, don't disengage for long. Gather energy and get back in the game. This part (your marriage) is actually more important than what you did all day.

Why can't she just sit and watch with me? That would be fun!

Yes, it would be—for you. Remember, men bond side by side, often in low-energy pursuits like watching things (games, shows, movies). Women tend to bond face-to-face with information exchanges. Find time and energy for some quality interaction doing what she loves and needs. This investment pays off in a big way.

What about kids? My guy friends tell me that babies change everything. And they don't sound completely enthralled.

It's true. Babies do change everything. Brace for the fact that you'll both be pretty weary and bleary-eyed during the first year. And she's working much harder at home than you are at work, even if the baby sleeps a lot. Be ready to relieve her at the end of the day. Again, negotiate together how you can help each other find recreation and do adequate self-care.

And remember, the baby is fun! And it's all worth it. And wives, it's tough, but save some energy for the kid's dad. Have fun!

laughter

CHAPTER 8

honesty

*Hiding, lying and posing
stand in the way of everything we want.
Let's get real.*

To begin the discussion about the next *building block,* honesty, consider the following scenario:

Betsy spends her entire day creating a new dish for Bob. She's poured her heart and many hours of labor into planning, shopping for, cooking and presenting this meal.

Bob comes home to an expectant wife. She's dancing with anticipation and coaxes Bob toward the glowing table to enjoy the feast that she's created.

With Betsy looking on, eyes bright and eager, Bob takes his first bite.

It's awful. Not okay. Not passable. A key ingredient is missing or else something nasty fell into the pot and died.

"Well?" prods Betsy. "Do you like it?"

Bob's initial expression could be perceived as deep delight and slow savoring, or it could be wretched suffering. He has only a moment to think.

What do I say? She's so excited. I don't want to hurt her; but I can't lie. She's going to taste it in a second, and she'll know I'm lying. And if by some quirk she likes it, then she'll make it again!"

Scenarios like this aren't make-or-break moments; but they illustrate the need for a shared approach to truth telling. When he asks, "Was sex good for you?" are you going to tell the truth if it wasn't? When she asks, "Do these pants make me look fat?" is there a good answer if they do?

STOP, TALK AND LISTEN

1. Have you had a similar "Bob and Betsy" moment? How did it turn out?
2. Would you have told the truth if you were Bob? How so?
3. Is it important to tell the truth, or are "white lies" a legitimate part of marriage?

Speak the Truth in Love

The Bible offers this telling proverbial advice: "[Speak] the truth in love."[19] That is the crux of the issue. If the truth is good news, don't withhold it. If the truth is hard news, then find a loving way to communicate it.

"Betsy," says Bob, "you've poured yourself into this meal and I love what you've done. For me, something about the flavor misses the mark; but you are amazing and I appreciate this."

Some would call that the sandwich approach—wrapping hard truth between two slices of affirmation. This is a very useful tool.

Others would call it ridiculous. "No one talks that way! If I don't like something, I just say it. It might hurt in the moment, but she has to toughen up!"

With respect to those "others," they are the most likely ones to suffer high conflict and increasingly painful marriages. Marriage requires skill. Skillful, thoughtful communicators tend to thrive; harsh, abrasive communicators tend to struggle. Speaking

---

19 Ephesians 4:15.

the truth in love is something to be practiced until we become highly skilled.

STOP, TALK AND LISTEN

1. Practice the sandwich approach around this truth: "The outfit you're wearing is not my favorite."
2. Did either one of you come from the Blunt Family? What are the aftershocks?

Seasoned Words

Still, we need to speak the truth. Withholding too much truth can be harmful in many ways. The other person might be harmed by falsehood and we can become embittered if we try to stifle all of our emotions or opinions.

So, hard truth requires seasoning. Hold it long enough to find the right words or the right moment. Create a context in a comfortable place at a time when your spouse is in a healthy way and a calm state of mind. Give a cue—a warning shot over the bow: "I have something difficult to say. Let me know when you're in the frame of mind to hear it." Pray for God's guidance and inspired timing. There must be a good way and a good time to deliver this truth.

STOP, TALK AND LISTEN

1. How are you at seasoning words to make them more palatable? Tell the truth about each other! (Good luck!)
2. Practice seasoning these words: "Last night's date was a boring waste of time."

---

honesty

How Much Is Too Much?

Dishonesty kills. It kills trust. It kills the intimacy that trust nurtures. And, eventually, it does terrible harm to respect.

We simply *must* tell each other the truth.

Are there no secrets? Can't we allow for some privacy?

Secrets? Not really. The word implies too much withholding. Privacy? Of course. We all have the right to keep our own counsel and harbor private thoughts.

There are some feelings and realities that are better kept between me and God. Other matters I entrust to a counselor or mentor or a close same-gender friend, and might not share with my wife. If we harbor too many of those untold truths, our intimacy will suffer. Still, we will always have our own private thoughts.

For example, my knee-jerk approach to work problems early in my marriage was to share them with my wife. She's a good listener and an insightful confidante. However, as I shared with her some of the pains and criticisms inflicted on me, her instinct to defend me rose up. And she had no outlet for that instinct. She couldn't fight my battles for me or reconcile frayed relationships that were mine (and others') to reconcile. In short, she was helpless. By telling her about these things, I only created stress for her, and even made it difficult for her to navigate relationships with people that she knew had strained feelings toward me.

Over time, I've learned to take my work troubles to others who can objectively sympathize or advise. And if I need a champion to rise up and defend me, it isn't my wife.

Does this filtering stunt intimacy? It could if I forget to tell her about my activities, hopes, goals and relationships at work. Remember that women build relationship primarily by exchanging intimate information—unlike men, who build relationship mostly by shared experience. So yes, I need to be somewhat forthcoming or else my wife will feel left out.

But again, season the truth in ways that lessen the blow and reduce the potential for creating undue stress.

STOP, TALK AND LISTEN

1. Can you remember a time when you probed for the truth and then wished you hadn't?
2. Do either of you feel *left out* of the other person's thought world? How does it make you feel?

Changeable vs. Unchangeable

Another piece of good advice came from the pastor who gave premarital counseling to my wife and me. "If something about the other person bothers you, and it's changeable, find a good way to encourage change. But if that thing bothering you is unchangeable, keep it to yourself and learn to accept it. This is *your* issue to manage privately. Telling the other person will only make her, or him, self-conscious and insecure."

For example, there might be a physical feature about your spouse that bothers you. If there is a reasonable course of action to suggest (exercise, wardrobe, diet, etc,) there might be a solution (I consider surgery unreasonable!). In other cases, that physical feature might be unchangeable—big nose, funny ears, freckles (Careful! I have a bunch!). Swallow hard, say a prayer and accept this imperfection. God knows, and you should know, you're not perfect either! So deal with it. You might even learn to love that unique feature over time.

Other things can be dealt with openly. When Sue and I married, my cleanliness habits were awful. I believe that I subconsciously married a woman who would bring order and cleanliness to my life. Early on, it must have been frustrating for her to cope with my messiness. Sometimes, she found productive ways to communicate her hopes for change. Occasionally, emotions erupted in one or the other of us. Often, she swallowed hard and prayed for my growth and change. I wanted change—really—for her and for me. Over the years, I've become much more ordered and it has benefited most aspects of my life. Her patience and care prevented this area from becoming a huge sore spot in our marriage. She was honest, but loving. She knew that I could change, so she told the truth about her hopes. But she didn't pester, mother or smother me, which would have caused a very negative and opposite reaction in me.

STOP, TALK AND LISTEN

1. Have you ever been told a criticism about an unchangeable characteristic that will forever stick in your craw?
2. Do you ever feel pestered or parented by your partner? Tell the truth in love!

Put Your Hopes on the Table

We must learn to communicate our hopes honestly. I can't meet my wife's needs if I don't know what they are. She can't come alongside my dreams if she doesn't know how I'm dreaming. And we have to practice the art of being honest about relational abrasions and bruises, or else we will keep scraping and bumping each other unnecessarily.

Occasionally, I'll be asked to intervene in a marriage where someone says, "I've been unhappy for a long, long time." And the other person cries, "How was I supposed to know? Why didn't you tell me?"

"I tried."

"Not hard enough."

"You should have known."

"I'm not a mind reader."

"You could have asked."

"You could have pulled me aside."

And so it goes. Don't get to that point! Ask. Tell. Probe. Share. Be transparent. Listen up. Develop the habit of telling the truth.

Not too much truth.

Not blunt truth in harmful ways.

Speak the truth in love. Wisely. Skillfully. Let's be honest with one another.

"What Ifs" and "What Abouts"

My partner is so quiet. I have to probe and prod and try to squeeze information out of him. It's frustrating.

Communicate your hope for a more forthcoming friendship. If you can't get him to disclose during engagement, the situation will likely be worse in marriage. Why? Because courting and engagement are all about disclosure; during that time, we tend to be at our best and boldest. Men tend to turn inward a bit after things get comfortable and, in their thinking, require less maintenance. "You already know me. Why do I have to keep talking?" Consider seriously whether you can marry someone who keeps his own counsel all the time. If you can, make sure you have a full stable of girlfriends to interact with.

honesty

My partner tells me everything. No filters. No discretion. Blunt. Abrasive.
Too much information!

Communicate your hopes for a better relationship. You probably can't lessen the flow of communication, but you can alter the blunt force of poorly chosen words. Again, make sure you can actually live with a person who is careless with words. During courting and engagement, behavior is usually at its best. Imagine that after the vows are spoken, still more filters will fall away. So you'd better encourage and negotiate real change before you find yourself in a very painful marriage. If that happens, then I'd be coaching you about how to toughen up and take it without constantly being bruised. In my opinion, that's no way to live; but some folks are able to endure a lot.

I have a secret or two. Things have happened that I know would hurt
my partner. But not telling hurts in a slow-burning way. What do I do?
Things heal in the light. Put it on the table and trust that your partner will gradually heal, forgive and accept the truth. Secrets are so toxic. Even if your partner never finds out, it's likely that there are suspicions. So it's eating away at both of you, undermining trust and delivering small doses of shame in you and fear in the other. Find the right time, place and words, and get it out into the fresh air. If you don't, it will turn putrid.

So should I be totally honest about all my past relationships?
No. Tell enough of the truth to prove that you're not living in the past. But you don't have to dredge up all the details. Tell the *general* truth about your previous relational and/or sexual history. Your partner deserves that much. But don't inflict on your partner specific images that will cause jealousy or fear.

CHAPTER 9

patience

I love you a lot.
Can you wait while I learn to love you well?
I'm slow, but I'm determined.

When premarriage couples compose their lists of *building blocks*, patience finds its way onto about half of the lists. If patience doesn't make the list, the couple almost always lands on a word or phrase that captures part of the meaning. And this seems to be what couples foresee:

> Marriage will require us
> to calm down when we feel like raging;
> to listen when we feel like talking;
> to stay when we feel like leaving;
> to be silent when we feel like screaming;
> to sympathize when we feel like fixing;
> to smile when we feel like grimacing;
> and to trust God with the overall development of
>   the other person.

Patience as Calmness

Patience as calmness is a skill that eludes some people. Since patience is a "fruit of the Holy Spirit,"[20] people who don't know God intimately will have difficulty accessing it. There is a

---

20 Galatians 5:22.

"peace ... which transcends all understanding" that "will guard your hearts and your minds in Christ Jesus,"[21] and if someone doesn't have Christ Jesus," this peace can seem foreign.

At the same time, calmness can be inherent in some temperament types, or as a result of growing up in a family climate that cultivated it. Some people seem predisposed to calmness, while others are wired to worry, emote and otherwise exude impatience.

STOP, TALK AND LISTEN

1. Is one of you, or are both of you, calm most of the time? What benefit does that bring to your relationship?
2. Where does that calmness come from? God? Family? Temperament? Experience?

When Things Are Anything BUT Calm

While some marriages can endure a lot of drama, it is generally true that uncontained emotions and unfiltered impatience strain most relationships. In the midst of unharnessed fireworks, it's common for accusations, name-calling and curses to fly unfettered.

Again, some people and couples can endure this, and might even report a purgative effect—or laugh about good make-up sex. But most will suffer if surging conflict characterizes their life together. Harmful words can't be retrieved. Physical violence breaks out when frustrations escalate and words land like bombs. After a few of these episodes, a relationship can go bad very quickly.

Somewhere, someone is reading this and saying, "But that's just how I am; and my family was the same way. What's wrong with it?"

21 Philippians 4:7.

Instead of "wrong," imagine that it is dangerous. Colorful, yes. Honest, too, perhaps to a fault. With lots of practice or with a third party present, maybe wild arguing has its place. But as a whole, calmness, self-control and the ability to keep a cool head will make a world of difference for the better.

Os Guinness writes, "The ability to control impulse is the base of will and character. Our passions, when well-exercised, have wisdom; they guide our thinking, our values, and our survival. But they all-too-easily go awry, and do so all too often."[22]

STOP, TALK AND LISTEN

1. Did either of you grow up in a highly conflictual household? What is the residual effect for you?
2. When you are angry, how well do your filters work? Why?

Personally Speaking

I know from firsthand experience. Sue and I entered marriage with a host of shared values and one quirky difference that made our marriage volatile. That volatility threatened our happiness in every way until we dealt with it (sometimes with outside help). In a nutshell, our difference had to do with managing intense emotion and conflict. While Sue is a calm and extremely nice person, she would have times when slights or misconstrued impressions would make her irritable. I brought a hypertuned sense of justice in concert with an insecure need for everything to be *all right, all the time*; couple that with a need to *be right* all the time. Our fights started, with Sue feeling frustration and me chasing out her feelings ("What's wrong?") only to be defensive and pompous when her feelings, in my opinion, "had no justifiable cause." Feeling unheard, she would become enraged; and feeling ill-used and attacked, I would become

---

22 Os Guinness.

unbearable, and the war would escalate to terrible levels. She'd get louder. I'd become laser sharp. We hurt each other badly.

We tried to tell friends that this was getting out of hand and that we were really suffering. People who knew us would say, "Oh, sure you fight. You're both so nice. Ken and Barbie! How bad could it be?" Honestly, they had no idea. Our neighbors knew! We knew. God knew.

We got help. We never quit working. We found counsel with God and others to get at our personal demons. Sue's irritability washed away, and her rages disappeared over time. My biggest lesson was to learn not to devalue her feelings, to let her express negative emotion without fixing or becoming defensive, and to get at the heart of why I was so obsessive about keeping the peace. And I had to learn to stop needing to be right all of the time.

Now we have moments and occasions of frustration or irritation, but we've learned skills that almost always resolve our squabbles before they escalate into an argument. I say "almost" because we've been humbled so many times that we'd be arrogant and nearsighted not to see the next argument looming—and to choose to handle conflict well. Now we go years between bad encounters, whereas we used to go weeks or even days between.

STOP, TALK AND LISTEN

1. Does any of this sound familiar? If yes, which parts? If no, why are you two different?
2. Is one of you more volatile? Both? Why? Family? Unresolved anger? Temperament?
3. How do you offset that volatility?

Figure Out What Works for You

This is what wellness looks like for us: if Sue feels irritation or frustration toward me, I'm learning to ask, "Is there something I can do, or is there something I need to hear?" If I'm not ready to hear, then it's not time to ask yet. When I'm ready, composed and calm, I ask.

If Sue is ready to talk, she does. If she isn't, I'm learning to allow her the space to sort her feelings and filter her anger, instead of coming unglued because of her emotion and igniting the fireworks by pressing and probing. Then, when Sue is ready to communicate, she does it much more calmly, and I try hard to contain any defensive impulses until I understand what she's experiencing. Occasionally I push back and tell my side of the story, but not in the whiny, defensive tones that used to be our undoing.

In short, we each own a personal process of learning patience and self-control. While everyone manages frustration, hurt and conflict in different ways, each person must find a pathway toward self-control.

And every couple needs to figure out what works for them. If the problem is icy calm without honest interaction, the couple needs to find ways to safely probe each other and communicate feelings. If the problem is a propensity toward physical altercation (this involves either men or women), a counselor should be called in right away to secure immediate safety, to unearth the causes and to create a pathway toward better anger management. If one person is a perpetual faultfinder and the other is ready to explode or escape, find a third party to help negotiate solutions. If cycles and escalating patterns of fighting badly are threatening the marriage, chart a course for breaking the cycle and seek help toward establishing better patterns.

Marriage involves skills. Skilled conflict managers have happier marriages—almost without exception. I say "almost" because

I know that there must be a couple somewhere that will report a twisted pleasure in battling constantly. I believe them when they say they're happy, but I wouldn't wish that kind of unrest on many people—and not just because I like everything to be "all right all the time."

STOP, TALK AND LISTEN

1. What works for you? When potential conflicts fizzle into mild disturbances quickly resolved, what makes it go well?
2. Identify in each other some skills that are helping you get through rough patches.

Patience as Waiting

Another aspect of patience is the art of waiting. All of us have to wait sometimes—stoplights, grocery store lines, Department of Motor Vehicles, doctor's offices. Waiting isn't easy.

The hardest part of waiting is this: waiting for your spouse to punch through a hard season. Of course, there are other chances to wait. Men will forever complain about waiting for their wives to add the last touch of makeup. Women will forever struggle with the wait when "he didn't get home when he said he would." Those stereotypical moments are the subjects of television sitcoms because they are so often real—and funny, if we let them be. But again, the harder waiting is for the life of the one we love to land in a better place.

Sue and I have taken turns suffering setbacks, physically and emotionally. From sports injuries and stressful seasons at work to times of real depression, my circumstances have forced Sue to wait on my return to full strength. From epilepsy to infertility to macular degeneration to breast cancer, Sue's body has malfunctioned in ways that have interrupted her yearning for a simple life. I've had to wait while she navigates every twist and turn.

Not that our waiting was passive. We were each involved in each others' wellness programs. But the one who waits has very little power to speed the healing process. And life is affected. Less energy. Less playfulness. Fewer romantic moments. Frustrations nearer the surface. Self-esteem battered by the inability to perform according to normal patterns and capacities.

These seasons test us in every way. They always test our patience.

STOP, TALK AND LISTEN

1. Do you have a hard time waiting? What's happening internally?
2. Has either of you had to wait for the other a lot? How does it make you feel?

So Where Do We Find Our Patience?

Again, patience is a fruit of the Holy Spirit. It grows more readily in lives that are yielded to God; true growth comes from having deep roots in that Father-child relationship.

And patience comes from being tested. The Bible says that our troubles actually work to our good as they grow perseverance and deepen character.[23] I don't wish hardship on anyone, but I've seen what people look like when they've been over-sheltered —it isn't very pretty. Troubles help to season us, and as they do they *can* deepen our love lives. I say "*can* deepen our love lives" because that deepening only happens if we hold on, stand firm in our commitments, and ride through hardship as full partners and friends.

---

23 James 1:2-4.

Every now and then, I hear stories of a marriage characterized by waiting. Sometimes life lands hard and one or both partners suffer badly and often. Every notion of a light, simple, playful marriage is turned upside down. This can be sad. It can also be the source of profound meaning and hearty growth and extreme pleasure and God-inspired devotion that might not be found in a carefree existence or a marriage that's untested by hardship.

Mostly, I wish you happiness. If you can't always be happy, I wish you patience and all its benefits. One of its benefits is wellness.

STOP, TALK AND LISTEN

1. If you are impatient, do you want to be more patient? If so, what curriculum do you have in mind? If not, why not?
2. It's hard to imagine the kind of life that requires you to love through calamity, but still … do you have the mettle to patiently endure a life that's completely different than your hopes? If not, what can you do to grow into a person with this kind of patience?

"What Ifs" and "What Abouts"

She has no respect for being prompt. We're late for everything!
It communicates so much disrespect to others. And to me!

Perhaps you learned the value of being on time and it's deeply ingrained in you. Perhaps she learned another value—the value of freedom from the controls and expectations of others. Even freedom from your tapping foot and obsessive clock watching.

Negotiate. Learn the value that she's indulging in and discover that there's something to be said for living in your own personal time zone. And then ask, "please," for the respect and kindness of being on time for a specific set of experiences. Communicate your hopes. "Honey, this is one of those meetings where tardiness would be very complicated. Is it possible that we could be a few minutes early?"

If she isn't willing, then you have a lot more talking to do. Why isn't she willing? Is passive-aggressive anger seeping out? Is she actually trying to hurt you, and why? Or is it just about clearing enough time for the rituals of preparing herself?

Me? What about him? He'll say he's coming home at six o'clock and he'll roll in at seven. Then, if I'm irritated, he acts like I'm being unreasonable.

Of course, sometimes there are legitimate problems that pop up and make people late. Usually, though, it's overreaching on the number of things we can accomplish in a day. Sometimes it's sloppy disciplines that leave us beckoning to the cry of even sloppier people—people who have planned so poorly that they also can't get home from work.

First, in the workplace, establish yourself as a person who works hard—very hard—but also values your home life. Don't try to present yourself as someone who'll do anything to get ahead, or else you'll be forced to live into your image.

Second, develop a ritual for closing the day that includes a strategy for tucking the undone matters away for tomorrow.

Leave yourself enough time—honestly—to get home when you said you would. Then, if you truly can't, it's an exception, not a norm. She'll give you grace.

CHAPTER 10

kindness

Little things
every day
because we both deserve to know
we're not forgotten.

L ike patience, kindness is a life skill as well as a marital *building block*. Yes, some people appear to be born kind. And some family cultures teach kindness with such proclivity that anyone raised in that environment will almost certainly be an absolute peach to marry.

For most of us, kindness is a learned behavior. For all of us, life itself is a journey from selfish preoccupation toward other-mindedness. Marriage pushes the curriculum of Kindness 101 into an advanced level course. We simply must learn kindness or else marriage is doomed.

First, kindness is a life bearing; a way of being. Kindness means thinking of the other person with fondness and eager curiosity.

"What would make her life better today?"

"What could I do to be truly helpful to him?"

I confess that entire days have passed by without ever asking how I can better my wife's life. Oh, I might have been available for this or that in ways that looked like kindness. But true kindness gives more. Kind people are not only flexible and available, but they're also creative and proactive.

STOP, TALK AND LISTEN

1. For tomorrow, write yourself a reminder. "Today, I'm going to make my partner's life better somehow." Then find a way.
2. What did you watch in your house growing up? Eager regard or passive disregard? Why do you think this was true?

Little Gifts, Little Deeds

One example is gift giving. I was fifteen years into marriage before I realized that gift giving is part of my wife's love language.[24] Before then, I'd seen how frugal she is, and I believed her when she selflessly said, "Don't spend any money on me!" What I eventually realized was that she thrives on gift giving and little kindnesses. I learned that stopping on the way home to buy her chocolate could be as effective as diamonds—more actually! When I stop to buy a gift, or when I bring something home from a trip, I'm declaring, "I never stopped thinking of you. You are always on my mind." And since most women—most people—enjoy being adored, gift giving is a great kindness.

Sometimes kindness takes mundane forms that send steady messages of love. For example, my wife and I started a toothbrush ritual early in our marriage that endures even during times of conflict. If Sue is the first one to brush her teeth, she prepares my toothbrush with toothpaste and leaves it beside the sink. If I'm first, I offer the same kindness. It doesn't happen every night, but with enough regularity to serve as a constant reminder—even when we've been arguing—that "I'm thinking of you."

---

24 Gary D. Chapman, *The Five Love Languages* (Chicago: Moody Publications), 1995.

When I think of my parents' marriage, I remember the little kindnesses. My dad helping my mom with her coat. My mom making meals in the morning and evening that were consistently good. My dad making coffee after every dinner. My mom doing laundry in and around all of her other commitments. While their marriage wasn't perfect, the model of kindness left a lasting imprint on me.

Because some of us did not grow up in a *Leave it to Beaver* household, kindness is a stretch. It may involve learning a whole new language.

STOP, TALK AND LISTEN

1. What's the favorite gift you've gotten from your partner? Why do you love it so much?
2. What's the favorite gift you've given to your partner? Why did you love giving it so much?

The Way We Word

As for words, we might be altogether unaccustomed to saying things in a kind way. If so, kindness is a critical skill that must be learned quickly. Abrasive tones and poor word selection batter a marriage with hurricane force. There is a huge difference between "You make me so mad, you jerk!" and "When things like this happen, I feel so frustrated!" The first comment is accusative and insulting and will always lead to defensive posturing and a counterattack. The second approach will likely be more well-received and won't spark a fire, even though it can carry just as much emotion.

We'll talk more about nonaccusative "I language" elsewhere. For now, know that saying something in a kindly manner makes understanding, dialogue and teamwork ten times more likely.

Ask for things kindly, sandwiched by "please" and "thank you." Proper manners were invented to smooth away rough edges and to lubricate the flow of relationship. If marriage becomes so comfortable that manners become unnecessary, look out! Just around the corner, the lack of courtesy will bite you.

Men, attention to kindness in word selection might feel like a steep, uphill run through a minefield. We aren't used to talking so carefully with each other. Then we marry and we're expected to be experts overnight! Honestly, though, didn't we woo our wives with kindly spoken affection? Now that she's your wife, it doesn't mean that you can quit wooing her.

STOP, TALK AND LISTEN

1. Name-calling and accusative language are brutal on a relationship. Do you have a proneness to do either or both?
2. Practice a nice way of saying, "You bug me so much! You left the toilet seat up again!"

Still to Pursue

A.W. Tozer writes about relationship with God, "To know him, yet still to pursue him; this is the soul's paradox of love."[25] The same goes for marriage. To know her and yet still to pursue her—this keeps marriage fresh and healthy. When we pursue women, we're not stupid enough to be unkind very often. If we were, she'd go away. If she was kind enough to marry you, why not continue to pursue her with kind words and kind gestures, assuming that you want her honest affection to continue?

Women, men *hate* to be pestered and bossed and nagged (of course, women don't like it either!). If you can't find a kind way to communicate your hopes positively, you will forever be

---

25 A. W. Tozer, *The Pursuit of God* (Rockville, MD: Serenity Publishers, LLC), 2008.

frustrated by his passive rebellion against helpfulness. Men *do not* marry their mothers. A man marries a friend and a lover. If you find yourself in a mothering role, move away from that role quickly! Rethink the way you ask for things, and you will likely see the end of his passive-aggressive hesitations. At the very least, you'll see more partnership around your hopes. He might not respond or participate as quickly or completely as you wish, but kind words will keep him in the game.

STOP, TALK AND LISTEN

1. Are you still pursuing each other? If so, how? If not, why not?
2. Do either of you ever feel mothered or fathered? How does it make you feel? What needs to change?

Affirm One Another

One form of kindness is affirmation. Again, the courting process is laden with words of appreciation. When we're dating, we say things that prove our affection. Too often, those words disappear in marriage as if affection were a given. It isn't.

One old joke illustrates this: A woman asks her husband, "Why don't you ever tell me you love me?"

His response: "I told you once. If anything changes, you'll be the first to know."

Bad joke; important message. Say it! Don't only say "I love you," but find the words to say *what it is* that you love. "How do I love thee, let me count the ways … ," wrote Elizabeth Barrett Browning. These are wise words and set an example for us to follow.

In our prayer lives, the experience is bumped up when we get beyond "Lord, I praise you" to "Lord, you are compassionate and merciful, faithful and powerful." As we reflect on the qualities in God that elicit praise, and find a language for it, our intimacy with God grows.

So it is with the language of love. Reflect on the qualities in your partner that you love and appreciate, and find a language for it.

Note to people who struggle with words: every effort you make will be doubly rewarding.

Those of us who are wordsmiths do well to learn other "languages," like acts of service, gift giving, physical touch and quality time.[26] If words come too easily, they might not carry as much force. I've learned that my loving soliloquies are not as effective for my wife as hanging a picture, vacuuming the house (unsolicited, even!) and taking the kids to the park to allow her some much-needed solitude.

STOP, TALK AND LISTEN

1. Do words of affection and affirmation come easily to you?
2. Are there other "languages" that communicate louder than words to you?

Kind Approaches to Tough Realities

One more thought on kindness. Sometimes, it's necessary to say something critical about the other person. Maybe a hurt is being suffered or an ongoing annoyance picks and pokes at contentment. If there really is the potential for change, honesty might demand that we speak our minds. Internalizing all of this negative emotion can also harm relationship, and even our health.

So what do we do? Find a kind way to tell the truth. Pick a context that softens the blow and choose words that frame the truth in love.

---

26 Gary D. Chapman, *Five Love Languages*. (Chicago: Moody Publications), 1995

Again, someone will argue, "You must be kidding! Why not just say it?"

The answer should be obvious. Kindness works. It's worth the extra effort and care.

"But what if I don't feel kindly toward my spouse? What if I'm bitter and angry and bugged and bothered?"

Without taking all responsibility away from your spouse, she or he is not personally responsible for the health and happiness of your frame of mind. If you're waiting for your spouse to deliver your sense of fulfillment and wholeness, you're waiting in the wrong line. Go to God. Dig deep. If necessary, get help to figure out what's bugging you. Unless this person you married has done a complete "Jekyll and Hyde" act, the major work that needs to be done is in you.

Pray for a kind heart and work hard at the ways of kindness. It will grow in you and on you.

So practice kindness. As I've said before, practice the way an athlete or artist practices a skill. Then you'll be able to practice the way a doctor practices the healing arts. Kindness is a practice that not only heals but prevents injury in the first place.

STOP, TALK AND LISTEN

1. Did you grow up in the Blunt Family, the Avoidance Family or somewhere in between?
2. Are you capable of being personally happy even if your partner is having a tough day? Why or why not?
3. Try making a list, even daily, of the aspects of your partner that make you thankful. No carryovers! Try to make a fresh list each day; then choose one quality to say out loud, "I was thinking today how thankful I am for the way you ..."

A Word of Warning

Some people are attracted to partners who are unkind. This is confusing and complex. Some people might not feel worthy of marrying a kind person, and subconsciously pursue a self-punishing relationship. Others are bored by kind people and pursue a sparring partner. Still others are sexually addicted to an unkind person, and the bodily connection makes breaking up almost undoable.

Please hear this: if you are on the verge of marrying an unkind person, get out now. You are walking into a horrible mistake that will be costly for years to come. You cannot change him. She isn't going to get nicer under the pressure of marriage. Really. Be smart. Pull out now. Kindness is that critical.

STOP, TALK AND LISTEN

1. Have you known a couple where one is sadly unkind to the other? What are your feelings and observations?
2. Do you ever feel emotionally *roughed up* by the other? Now is the time to talk about it.

"What Ifs" and "What Abouts"

What about comfortable love? I mean, I didn't marry her so that I'd have to constantly work, work, work on a relationship. Why can't we just accept each other the way we are and grow old together? Why can't she stop trying to improve me and tweak us?

This is a common male question. Since men tend to choose low-maintenance friendship as the ideal, we transfer that expectation into marriage. Guess what? Most women aren't built this way. Even their female friendships are active; women press each other for quality time and substantive growth in relationship. Face it. You're the one that gets to *accept* what is— a dynamic relationship that will stretch you beyond comfort.

Kindness is good, but can't we be real? I mean, can we pass gas in front of each other? We don't have to be pleasantly polite all the time, do we?
Of course you can be real. But know that reality bites. The home is a place to heal from the pains and strains of life in the bigger world. So more gentleness, kindness and care will be nurturing. And, frankly, too much crass reality can douse the flame of romance. Best to keep a few mysteries alive. And a woman will usually want to be treated like a lady.

I'm the one who practices all the kindness. He grew up in a home where his dad did all the receiving and his mom did all the giving. It seems like it's in his DNA to be waited on by a woman.
Good luck. If you're one of those people who *loves* to serve others hand and foot, you might be very happy. Some people aren't happy unless they're fawning all over others and feel the sense of self-importance that comes from being the sole care-giver. It's weird to me, but if that's you, go for it.

If you aren't a glutton for punishment, take action now. If you're married, get a counselor and get to work on a better way of interrelating. If you're not married, postpone or cancel the wedding until you're sure that you're marrying a man and not an emotional infant.

But he's just old-fashioned. His contribution is to provide and protect! My job is to serve and nurture!
Okay, it sounds like you really are the fawning type. Today, it might sound fun and fine. I'm just trying to warn you that years down the road it might start feeling a bit unfair. You also deserve to be treated kindly.

kindness

understanding

You're a mystery to me and a moving target.
Help me,
and I'll keep pursuing you all of my days.

This may be a bit surprising to hear, but the outcome of every good fight is not agreement; it's understanding. Agreement might not be possible. Nor may victory for one over the other, which only leaves the other feeling beaten down and pushed away. Not even peace, since peace without understanding is a thin Band-Aid® with adhesive that's not very sticky.

True understanding will lead to something better than agreement; it will lead to respect. Understanding will spread the victory to both sides. And understanding will bring a kind of peace that is more informed and more stable.

Let's say that the flames of conflict are burning hot. The sooner we can get to the point of really listening and actually caring about what we're listening to, the sooner the conflict will be resolved. We're on a quest to harness our negative emotions enough to honestly ask, "Please, what are you really feeling? And I'll do my best not to react."

Again, the process of truth telling is greatly aided by non-accusative "I" language. "I'm feeling abandoned and lonely" is a much more effective communication than "You've deserted me and left me out in the cold, you lousy...." Understanding happens when I say, "This is what I'm feeling . . ." or "This is what I'm experiencing . . ." or "This is how it looks from my angle . . ." or "This is how my mind works. . . ." "I'm not asking you to agree, and I'm not saying that I'm right. But this seems to be my reality. . . ."

Some people will cry, "You must be kidding. That's not how I talk!"

Correct. I understand. And when Picasso was young, he probably finger painted. Working together toward understanding is an art form. You both can become adept at this kind of communication, and the sooner the better. Groove these patterns of communication and you will enjoy being in one of the small minorities of marriages that are virtually conflict-free.

Conflict-free? Yes. Once understanding is achieved, acceptance and respect follow fast on the heels. As long as we're not completely forgetful of what we've learned about the other, we're much more likely to avoid the affronts that lead to conflict.

STOP, TALK AND LISTEN

1. Do you have an overactive need to be right when you argue? Any idea why?
2. Can you imagine a marriage free from harsh conflict? Does it appeal to you? Why?

It Took Me Years!

For example, it took years for me to understand something very simple about my wife and about me. Once I understood it, life became so much easier. Here it is: sometimes I'm annoying. Not intentionally, but actually.

When my wife registered annoyance, I would react badly for two reasons. First, I didn't know I was being annoying. And, second, I'm not someone who is prone to being annoyed.

Here's the kicker: the one thing that tends to annoy me is when people get annoyed.

So imagine our dilemma. She occasionally got annoyed. I couldn't understand her annoyance and was annoyed that she was annoyed. I behaved in morally superior and defensive ways.

Before this story gets too annoying, let me say that I finally learned the value of letting my wife feel whatever she needs to feel; instead of reacting badly. Her annoyance was usually short-lived and often justified. I learned to ride it out and, gradually, to trim away at the things that she found annoying. I even learned that sometimes, not always, her annoyance was tied to other events, emotions and even body chemistry. During those times, I learned to *let her be* instead of trying to change her feelings or fix her, and things just cleared up more quickly. Understanding made all the difference.

Sue is a very conciliatory person, and she always apologizes for her part. Her annoyance has greatly diminished and I have learned to glean from those moments whatever behavior on my part either contributes to her frustration or helps her to get past it.

In other words, instead of fighting her feelings, I gradually have learned to be her partner *through* whatever it is that's plaguing her. I've come to accept that she (like most women) is far more complex than I am—emotionally and even chemically. And I've come to respect her for the way she fights down the tides of emotion that can threaten to darken her day.

STOP, TALK AND LISTEN

1. Is one of you more easily annoyed? What happens?
2. Are you gaining understanding of how to avoid or dissipate those annoyances together?

understanding

It's Tied to Trust

Obviously, some of this understanding is made possible by a growing trust. Early in the marriage, the annoyance or frustration of one partner can be frightening to the other.

"What if she leaves?"

"What if he doesn't love me anymore?"

"What if I've ruined everything?"

Over time, and after a few battles, we usually see enough evidence to believe that the other person won't leave (right?) and that we can relax and come alongside if our partner is having a bad day.

People are complex. Keep learning! Keep asking questions, probing and prodding to the point of understanding. Dare to listen to hard truth and even to invite it: "Is there anything that I do, or don't do, that can frustrate you?" Communicate mutual hopes for growth and improvement, and be patient and gracious. People are a slow-growth forest!

And when people do change, it isn't always in the direction we were hoping for. Adapt. Pursue the ever-changing person in front of you with relentless curiosity. Curiosity might have killed the cat, but a *lack* of curiosity kills marriage. Ask questions. Keep talking. Listen like crazy. Don't assume. Turn over every stone. Learn.

STOP, TALK AND LISTEN

1. Do you ever wonder or worry that the other will simply quit and walk out? Why? Help each other.
2. Have you ever been surprised by a change in your partner? How did the adapting go?

Curiosity Is Not, by the Way, Control

Every impulse to control the other person will cause your partner to close up like a clamshell. No one likes to be controlled. Even the most submissive personalities will close in and close us out if we behave in controlling ways. If efforts at understanding become an exercise in "knowing therefore controlling," then intimacy will break down.

Let me go further: the exchange of information causes intimacy to grow. The exchange of deep, heartfelt information makes intimacy grow deep. As we probe one another and peel away layers of protection through the brave practice of transparency, we become ever-more-linked. It's much like sex, frankly. We get naked together and probe into deep, previously impregnable regions. This builds intimacy. And trust. And understanding.

So we're pretty vulnerable now. Extra care is required. Again, not manipulation or control. Intimate information isn't ammunition for the next fight, or else the door to closeness will slam shut again.

By the way, men will often have a hard time reading this information on intimate exchange. Why? Men tend to gauge intimacy more on shared experience than on shared information. That's why a man can spend a whole day golfing with a close friend and return home with absolutely no information.

"How's Joe's wife?" asks Mary.

"I forgot to ask," says Mike.

"How's his job?" she asks.

"I didn't want to bring it up," he answers.

"Are his kids back in school?"

"Never got to the kids."

"Did they buy that house?"

"What house?"

"What did you talk about?" she asks, getting frustrated.

"Not much, I guess," he answers.

"And you call yourself friends?" she half spits.

"No, we call ourselves *best* friends," he says honestly, not understanding the tone of the question. Why? Because men feel closest (usually) to those with whom they share experiences, and not necessarily information.

STOP, TALK AND LISTEN

1. Does one of you tend to dig? Does one of you tend to withhold? How does it work when it works best?
2. Have you had an experience like Mike and Mary? Reflect on it.

Men, Women, and Information

It can be frustrating for women that men are not always more forthcoming with personal information. It can be equally frustrating that men do not tend to probe for personal feelings and details. As mentioned before, since this is the greater part of female relationship-building, it can be confusing to women when men show limited interest in this fundamental behavior.

Women, you must understand this and work toward acceptance of this fact—your husband may be a novice in this realm of mutual disclosure. And try to accept this—he's just not as curious as you are about details. Be patient and hopeful, and be honest about your need for this kind of sharing in order to feel close.

Men, you must understand this fundamental female appetite for personal information. And you need to practice participating. The rewards are numerous for her and for you. Yes, it feels risky to disclose personal information. You might not even want to *think* about these matters. But good communication in relationship requires you to rehash these things out loud. And the sorting and sifting and lamenting (*not* problem solving!) that's common to female communication will make you both closer.

A woman might say, "Duh! He doesn't know this?"

The answer, in a word, is No. Men tend to live a compartmentalized existence where different arenas of life are carefully separated. A female therapist explained it to me this way: "Men are like file cabinets. Open a drawer. Pull out a file. Work that problem. Replace the file. Close the drawer. Open another drawer. Women tend to be more integrative. All files are carefully placed on the table with every corner touching."

So men tend to be *where they are* and not where they aren't. Women tend to be everywhere at once in a sophisticated network of awareness. We joke about women, not men, as multi-taskers and we are generally accurate.

STOP, TALK AND LISTEN

1. Why do men tend not to lament? Any idea why men tend to explain away each other's problems instead of empathize?
2. Does the "file cabinet" conversation fit in your case, or are you different than the stereotype?

The Ideal Date

Again, the sooner we accept and even respect these differences, the better off we are.

The ideal date, by the way, will involve a segment of face-to-face personal sharing and another segment of side-by-side experiential sharing. Dinner and a show, or a ballgame and then coffee, or a picnic and a hike, will allow both fundamental approaches to intimacy to be satisfied.

Or, most men would admit under duress, dinner and sex, or coffee and sex, or a picnic and sex—any of these options works. Like it or not, sex is an experience that most men report to be the most powerful way to create closeness. Like it or

understanding

not, most women would place sex somewhere down the line. Understanding this difference, and learning to accept and even respect it, is very important.

Yes, men can make it seem like personal sharing is little more than foreplay. It might seem that way because, for typical men, it's true—personal sharing is foreplay.

"Does it always have to be that way?"

No. Get it, guys? Sharing doesn't have to lead to sex.

But ladies, realize that sex is where his mind is moving. Ignore or neglect that very natural movement and you will be shutting him out as surely as if he decided to quit talking and listening.

"But that makes me feel controlled and manipulated—even used!"

Hear that, men? Please understand.

All across the board, please understand. Dare to know and be known. Dare to describe what it feels like to be you; and dare to listen and imagine what it feels like to be the other person.

"What Ifs" and "What Abouts"

What if he lacks curiosity about my life? He makes my relationships feel trivial and my activities constantly devalued.

Share how you feel. "I feel devalued sometimes. My day isn't treated with interest or curiosity. What do I do with these feelings?" If he's a thoughtful person at all, he'll probe for more feelings and practice new behaviors. Now, be patient. This can be slow growing for guys.

We fight until we're exhausted. She can't lose. She's tenacious. I'm so tired.
Ask for space somewhere in the conflict. Give a reassurance that you aren't leaving, but communicate your need to rest and collect your thoughts. Then reengage. At some point, it might be good to say, "I'm comfortable agreeing to disagree. Is there anything about disagreement that feels threatening to you? Help me understand." Or you can ask, "Do you need to win this argument? If you do, that's fine. But can we find a win-win?" The first part might sound a bit confrontational, but that's not all bad.

She's an ever-moving target; a mystery to me. When I think I have her figured out, she changes again.
This is a common lament for men, if you can get men to lament. The dynamic reality of womanhood isn't familiar to men. Guys are accustomed to static relationships and cautious about other men who create drama. But just because that drama is unfamiliar doesn't make it bad. Learn to understand and embrace the complexities of the *sophisticated* gender and celebrate the spice that she brings to your life. Remember, you're learning to play a violin, not a tuba! Have you seen how violinists have to retune the instrument after almost every movement?

CHAPTER 12

acceptance

Do you love who I am or who you want me to be?
God knows I'll try to grow.
Still …

With growing understanding, acceptance is often the next step. Now that I know my spouse more, with warts and pimples included, can I make peace with this emerging picture? Now that I see better what makes my partner's machinery tick, and what makes it shut down, can I accept this person that I love "for better or for worse?"

This is difficult for many people. Numerous conversations indicate that acceptance is stereotypically or typically tougher for women. While every conversation regarding stereotypes is bound to surface exceptions, it appears that women are often the *keepers* of relational health. Women appear to be more acute in their perceptions about the things that disrupt relational flow and tend to feel these disruptions more deeply. It seems that women can be more exacting with a higher level of expectation in their friendships as a whole. All this to say, it is much more common to have a woman in my office frustrated with her husband than to have a man in my office lamenting over his wife.

Part of that phenomenon could be communication patterns. It's more common for men to go inward with frustration and for women to go outward. Female lamentation is normal and can

acceptance

129

be a central portion of conversation between women (who, as you'll remember, create intimacy by personal sharing); whereas men tend to fix each other, mock each other and generally talk dismissively when one ventures out to express a woe. [27]

But there's more here than mere communication. Men tend to be *laissez-faire* in their approach to relationships. A *best* friend is usually an *easy* friend. In marriage counseling, men tend to communicate frustration primarily regarding the frustration level of their wives. "She's never satisfied!" To put it simply, most men hunger for uninterrupted peace at home, in part because *experiencing* life side by side is already deemed intimate; even if there is no deeper, face-to-face sharing. Women, on the other hand, report the loss of intimacy that can be the result of a husband's *laissez-faire* approach; a lack of intentional relationship-building equals relational slippage.

STOP, TALK AND LISTEN

1. When you are frustrated, do you tend to go inward, outward or both?
2. Which one of you is more likely to assess relational health and comment about the need for change?

Marrying a "Project"

In lighter terms, perhaps you've heard this quip: Women go through life wishing their husbands *would* change; men go through life wishing their wives would *never* change.

Some of this hunger for improvement in a woman must be good, but it can make acceptance difficult. It will forever be necessary for most women to lament out loud to a friend or family member about a dissatisfying aspect of marriage.

---

27 Deborah Tannen, *You Just Don't Understand: Women and Men in Conversation* (New York: William-Morrow Publishers), 1990.

The best friend and the wise family member will respond with more than mere sympathy. Someone needs to say, "Do you love that man for who he is or do you love him for who you want him to be?" However unfair, the stereotype is that women can marry men whom they view as worthy "projects." There are a host of jokes and tales and movies and sitcoms that follow this theme into particulars that amount to this: "He had better change or else."

My counsel is this: she had better change her appetite for change or else she's going to be miserable. And if your marriage turns out to be the flip-flop of the stereotype, then he has this same work to do.

STOP, TALK AND LISTEN

1. Ask each other, "Are you in love with who I am or with who you want me to become?" Answer honestly.
2. Now ask your partner, "Could you be happy if I remained fundamentally the same person for the rest of our lives?" If so, why? If not, explain.

The Old Bait and Switch

Let me sympathize, then problem solve. Female or male, part of the heartbreak is "the old bait and switch." During the dating and courting process, couples are on their best behavior. This is not deception—it's our earnest attempt to win the affection of someone to whom we're attracted. But once that prized partner has been won, relaxation is understandable. Behaviors intended to win the day seem less necessary; certainly less urgent. Since no emerging relationship is a done deal until the wedding day, the special kindnesses often gear back and fall away immediately after the wedding. This is where disappointment can set in—fast and heavy.

acceptance

Here are the disappointments I hear most. From the young wife, "He used to look at me like I was the center of the universe. He'd call me, surprise me, bring me gifts and hold my hand. When we got married, his damned job became the center of his universe and I now get the leftovers. Did he do all of those nice things just to get me to marry him?"

From the man, "Before we were married, she was affectionate —I mean, really affectionate. She actually even seemed to like me and want my body. Then when we got married, someone flipped a switch. Now she acts like she's doing me a favor when we make love. Was that all an act before we were married?" Men actually joke, "What's the best medicine for a nymphomaniac? Wedding cake."

No, it wasn't an act. And no, he didn't woo you by being false.

Things change. Rather, things that we wish would never change *do* change. And the change we wish for happens ever … so … slowly.

STOP, TALK AND LISTEN

1. Can either of you foresee a bait-and-switch coming? From you? From the other? Talk about it.
2. Can you identify a bait and switch that you feel has already happened? Why or why not?
3. What kinds of bait-and-switches would be very devastating for you? Why?
4. Why do some men (or women) shut off gifts and courtesies after marriage? Why do some women (or men) lose sexual interest? Do we fight these tendencies or just accept changes like this?

You Are Who You Are

Part of the solution lies in forgiveness, which is another chapter. The piece we'll deal with here is acceptance. "He is who he is; upsides and downsides. I married him for better or for worse." And "She is the woman I married, even though she is a person who is always evolving."

That really is the truth. From the viewpoint of a husband, a woman is an ever-evolving mystery. Before marriage, he might have hints of this, but during courtship she probably presents in a more consistent way. After marriage, loving her is like trying to hit a moving target. Natural monthly cycles and the ebbs and flows of life seem to sweep over a woman with the force of nature's seasons. Most men are not only geared differently; they are allergic to this kind of sea change.

Why? On a Myers/Briggs personality study, eighty percent of men register as *thinkers* over *feelers* (T over F).[28] This doesn't mean that men have no feelings. It means that eighty percent of men (and twenty percent of women) use rational thought to trump feelings. Feelings matter, but they are superseded by rational logic. Men don't trust or honor feelings as much. A man might say, "I might feel lousy today, but it is irrational for me to allow my feelings to affect anyone around me. So, it's time to *suck it up*." Most men do this either by nature or by training, since there are very few places where a man can go to hear any other message—either from men or from women. Even women communicate their wish that "he would be stable, a quiet listener and pretty much okay all the time. When he's out of balance, it scares me."

For better or worse (I'm using that phrase a lot in this chapter quite on purpose), either naturally or by training that starts early in life, men learn how to ignore feelings and remain constant regardless of emotions. Most men are told to be "the rock," either by internal or external voices.

---

28 Ibid.

Unfortunately, rocks aren't very pliable. Maybe my wife wishes that I hadn't been *set in stone* until she had a chance to do a bit more shaping.

But here's the upside—I'm like an anchor through her storms. I haven't been perfect, but my relatively unchanging nature has been a huge comfort to my wife during seasons of crises. My crises have tended to happen in a season of exhaustion *after* her worst crises—that's something to watch for and be cautious about. And she certainly showed up with strength during my crises. But she would admit that the emotional frequencies for her and most women are set much differently. There's little in my experience or reading that would alter that view. Again, there *are* exceptions and role reversals.

STOP, TALK AND LISTEN

1. Does any of this *thinking over feeling* talk make sense? How do you think or feel about the way most men are wired?
2. Which one of you is "the rock" in the relationship? Why do you think ... or feel ... it is that way?

Stop Trying to Fix Her

On a Myers/Briggs test, if eighty percent of men tend to be thinkers, then eighty percent of women (and twenty percent of men) prove to be *feelers* over *thinkers* (F over T). That doesn't mean *feelers* don't think or that *feelers* lack intelligence. It simply means that feelings are more trusted internally, are more influential and are more likely to trump rational reflection. Feelings have much more power to dictate behavior and mood.

Most men view this as irrational, perilous and nonsensical. When the wife begins to communicate negative emotion, it's not uncommon to hear a man say, "Snap out of it! Can't you just let it go? Are you *trying* to be hurt and angry? Am I supposed to hop-to just because you're in another one of your moods?"

The response? "You don't understand, you unfeeling so-and-so! Quit trying to fix me. I can't and I won't snap out of it! I *am* hurt and you can't wish it away."

Because he does "wish it away" as a matter of routine in his own internal world, he really can't understand why she can't or won't. Because she can't or won't wish it away, she really can't understand why he would be so dull and unfeeling.

Men, the huge upside of a woman's proneness is this: as she leaves her emotions on the table they are actually *dealt with,* instead of being stuffed away. Learn from her and you might find healing yourself; and you might even avoid high blood pressure and a heart attack. Internalizing emotion has its functional side and its dangerous side.

STOP, TALK AND LISTEN

1. Which one of you is the *feeler*? How do you know?
2. How do each of you cope with deep fears, worries and frustrations? Verbally? Inwardly? Publicly? Privately?

Viva la Difference

Here's the crux: these differences can work *for us.* There are times when it is really helpful to have a *feeler* in the house. And there are moments—even seasons—when having an unfeeling rock can be a source of great security. Accept one another! Celebrate your differences. Rely on the fact that God made you and your partner on purpose.

Men, accept your wives! Yes, they might be subject to a host of ill winds that shift them like weather vanes. So be it! They keep your life interesting, colorful and well-applied. You get to

acceptance

be a rock and a protector for someone you love. Most of us are built for that. And you get to practice the arts of listening and sensitivity. You might even learn how to sort through your own emotions with more dexterity. Your wife is mysterious and sophisticated. You get to spend your whole life figuring her out.

Women, accept your husbands! Some of us are hard and simple and clumsy and entirely clueless about the complexity of your feelings. But isn't it good, in an ever-changing world, to have someone steady and dependable? And you get to color his world by being mysterious and sophisticated!

Laugh about this weird and wonderful quirk in God's creation. Quit trying to pretend that sameness is better. If you need someone to be the same, or close to it, foster a same-gender friendship. Revel in your marriage for what it is—complimentary.

"What Ifs" and "What Abouts"

Honestly, I'm a pretty good guy. Not perfect, mind you, but I have a lot of upsides. She started with my grooming and now she's trying to change my core personality. What do I do?

Ask her for one curriculum—one thing she'd like you to work on—per six-month season. Then really try to serve her hopes by applying yourself. Maybe she does know best and the change might make you both happy. Try not to be embittered about it. Knowing that you're trying without scorn will touch her heart.

He doesn't understand me or accept my feelings. Instead of coming alongside, he tries to make me think like him; which pretty much means he wants me to live in denial of my deeper self.

Yes. He doesn't understand. But he probably will learn to accept the complexity of your life. Occasionally, thank him for listening and remind him how useful sympathy can be. You just need a partner, right? Someone who isn't trying to judge or fix you when feelings get disjointed. This is new behavior for most men. Give him time to develop some relational muscles.

But I just want peace! The world is tough enough. When I get home, I want to rest, not answer to a host of accusations about how I'm not doing enough.

Get real. You're married now. You share life with a human being with real hopes and needs. Brace up. Grow up. Practice new behaviors. Figure out how to ask for the pockets of rest that you need. Then enter the fray. It's worth it!

But I hate being a nag! I don't even like the sound of my own voice when I accuse and prod and whine.

Then don't nag—not ever. Find positive ways to communicate hope in a tone that welcomes partnership. Use "I" language, not accusative words: "I love it when …" "It's difficult for me whenever …" Whining is very unappealing and unattractive behavior.

And do some personal inventory. *Why am I asking for change? Maybe the change needs to happen in me?*

Honestly, I'm married to a malcontent. I don't think anything ever will satisfy. Life is one disappointment and drama after another. What do I do about my spouse?

First, you might need to accept this as an unchangeable. Unless your spouse seeks help, you could live the rest of your life with this person and this reality.

Second, find contentment yourself—and don't base your happiness on your spouse. Base it on the unchanging love and power of God. The apostle Paul wrote to the Philippian church that he'd found the secret to contentment, even as he wrote from prison. He'd learned the secret of being happy "in plenty or in want." He wrote, "I can do everything through him who gives me strength."[29] Cultivate a strong relationship with Jesus and enjoy the ever-increasing benefits.

Third, look for the right moment and manner to intervene or confront your spouse. "From my perspective, I see unhappiness and a steady stream of disappointments. I hope you, and we, don't have to live this way forever. Is there something we can do; someone we can talk to? Will you walk with me on a path to something better?"

If the answer is "no," you might be searching for your own contentment in a marriage that threatens to be a kind of prison. But it doesn't have to be. Nurture the marriage all of your days and find your nurturing wherever you can get it. I believe that God has special rewards in heaven for those who have been long-suffering and courageous.

My spouse is a nag. Nothing I do is right. It's wearing me down.
If you can muster the courage, you can actually coach and support your spouse's approach to things. "I feel bossed and I feel corrected. Since I'm not an employee or a child, I'm curious about ways to improve our communication and actually help realize your hopes." Involving your spouse in this discovery process might actually help, especially if you aren't digging in your heels as if to say, "I'm not doing *anything* you tell me to do." Your spouse might have some genuine hopes that might be worth realizing together.

And there is nothing wrong with saying, "I don't take orders and I heard you the first time. If I heard a more encouraging tone, I might even be eager to help."

---

29 Philippians 4:13.

But I've tried being nice. My spouse never does what I ask. I wait and I wait. Nagging feels like the only solution.

Try reaching some understanding. "I feel as if I communicate my hopes gently and my hopes are ignored, or procrastination leaves me waiting and waiting. Sometimes I feel like nagging is the only way to get help, but I don't want to nag. Can you help me? Is there something I don't understand?"

The answer will likely come back, "I'm so sorry, etc." But you might also receive some very helpful information. Maybe there are actual reasons for procrastination and if you can flush out some passive-aggressive motives, resolution of anger could bring lasting help.

Some of you are married to, or marrying, unhelpful people. There must be something meritorious about them or you wouldn't be together. If you're bound to someone who simply isn't wired to be helpful, then get used to this: you will either be doing the work yourself or hiring it out. Any gains or improvements by your spouse are likely to be gradual at best.

I don't feel accepted. There are things about my core person that my partner doesn't like. I'm coming undone. If affects my self-esteem and ruins entire days.

If you're married, get help. If you aren't, get out. If you're being asked to change something that's *unchangeable,* then you both need serious help in, or out, of relationship—depending on whether you are married or not.

The following seems so obvious, but love and sexual ties can blind us. If your partner doesn't build you up, don't marry that person. In the best love relationships, I don't only feel good about my partner; I also feel good about *myself with my partner.* I don't only feel love for my wife. I also love who I am when I'm with her.

CHAPTER 13

respect

You are God's workmanship—a work of art.
There's no one else like you.
He has sacred plans for you
and I intend to help see them through.

Acceptance is a wonderful thing. But respect is even better. It's good and fine to arrive at a point of accepting the pros and cons, costs and benefits, ups and downs of the person you married. Acceptance means peace for you and settledness for your household.

Respect means so much more. It means that there is something truly honorable and praiseworthy about your spouse. Respect means that you hold him or her in a place of high regard. "Something about *who you are* continues to impress me. I think of you as an extraordinary person."

Actually feeling this way and then giving expression to that respect is crucial. Conversely, the loss of that sense, coupled with the failure to communicate respect, is catastrophic in a marriage.

The problem, of course, is that we disappoint each other. Respect suffers body blows. During courtship, we're mostly able to sustain our best impulses and refrain from our worst ones, creating an incomplete projection of who we really are. I'm not suggesting that we lie or intentionally deceive during courtship; we simply rise to the occasion and put our best foot forward. After we're married, life happens. Shared space and special circumstances bring out less-than-stellar sides of us. The close-up view can uncover flaws and foibles of every kind. This can be disconcerting—even deflating. Respect is damaged when the other person deflates right in front of our eyes.

STOP, TALK AND LISTEN

1. Why is respect so important?
2. Do each of you feel respected by the other? How so?
3. Have you ever been deeply disappointed in a relationship? If so, how? If not, do you fear such a thing?

The First Tonic—Realism

Surprisingly, one of the best tonics for disrespect is popping a bubble of delusion with stark realism. Did you really think she'd be perfect? Did you honestly believe he'd have no dark sides or rough edges? Are you truly that naïve? People *are* that naïve, and that's only one out of a host of flaws that *will* surface.

While there's nothing wrong with dreaming about Prince Charming, even Prince Charming makes obnoxious bodily noises when he's off camera. And while there's nothing wrong with hoping for a woman who's the *whole package*, there are some throw-ins in the party bag that might interrupt the party.

So get real! Get over it! Good morning, it's a new day! Wake up and go to school. Learn how to adjust your focus and bring yourself into alignment with reality. This is not her problem; it's yours. He is not responsible for making your dreams come true; you are responsible for bringing your hopes into the realm of reality. She didn't trick you; you were fooled by your idealism. He didn't do a bait-and-switch; you made the mistake of being delusional. No one's perfect but Christ alone, and even

Jesus can be hard to live with! Have you ever tried to live with someone who's perfect?

Obviously not, and that's the point. Your partner is imperfect. You're not perfect either, so live with it. I mean that literally. Live with her. Live with him. This is the person God has given you. This is the person you have chosen. Let go of the regrets before they become toxic. This is it. Deal with it. Grieve a bit, if you have to. Now get on with it!

Are there exceptions—cases so bad that an annulment is the order of the day? Rarely, but yes, if a violent streak comes out, or criminal involvement, or anything so completely twisted that life together becomes immediately unimaginable. I've known of a case where sex was promised in marriage and then completely withheld. I almost *never* suggest divorce, but early annulment makes sense when something absolutely weird has been hidden during engagement and exposed in marriage.

But for almost all of us, marriage exposes us in more ordinary terms. Annulment or divorce is *not* the answer when our weaknesses surface. If it was, no one would stay married. Most ceremonies include a semblance of these words: "for better or for worse" and "in sickness and in health." Do we mean it? If we do, we need to hold to it.

STOP, TALK AND LISTEN

1. Is either one of you an idealist? Are your bubbles easily burst?
2. Do you feel like you know each other well enough? Have you flushed out all of your weird secrets? If not, do tell!

My Own Curriculum

As I've mentioned before, my own marriage was painfully conflictual in the first year. While much of the tension was based on ordinary differences and frictions, we also suffered

respect

one enormous shock—my wife's rage. Again, we were both shocked by it. While I own every contributing factor in the ordinary course of conflict, Sue's extraordinary rage startled both of us within a month of our wedding. Our vows were tested immediately. We knew that we loved each other a lot, but we also knew that our conflict patterns would ruin our relationship.

Our marriage was saved by two things. First, Sue was genuinely remorseful and utterly committed to finding the root causes of her rages. Her respect for me, for herself and for God made the rages incompatible with every other facet of our lives.

Secondly, my respect for her grew in leaps and bounds. Not because she was perfect. Her healing process was a slow climb with notable setbacks. My respect surged with her courage and tenacity. Every causal discovery proved what a survivor she is and every step of progress showed me portions of her character that I might never have seen. She earned my profound respect, even *more so* because of the hard experiences we endured together.

And I have her respect. She watched my resilient commitment to forgiveness and my eagerness to put each setback into the past.

My point? Respect can be born from unexpected places, even out of real weakness and pain. Perfection isn't one of those places. That's reality. Live in it.

STOP, TALK AND LISTEN

1. Some respect is born through the labor of a personal battle. Have you already had a major battle or two that have forced you to be a bigger, better person and/or a stronger couple?

Tonic Number Two—Curiosity

Another tonic that grows respect is curiosity. "Who are you, really, and what is God doing with your life? How are you growing and becoming and evolving under the influence of God and the seasons of life?"

Picture a garden with a variety of colors, shapes, aromas and potentials season to season. Respect is that careful curiosity that watches, wonders and steps softly through the garden. No tromping. No ignoring. These emerging qualities and budding possibilities are tender; even fragile. It's not a French garden with clear lines, marked pathways and ordered growth. It's more of an English garden, growing here and there in absurd disorder that creates an overall effect that's much more promising.

Why do we tromp heavily at times? Why do we disrespect the other? First, as I said earlier, failed promises or fallen dreams can burst our bubbles. But we also disrespect our spouse because of a clumsy inattention to what's really happening in the other person. And, in turn, the other feels a resulting soreness from that clumsiness.

One critical thing to remember is that adult life is a lot harder than childhood or adolescence. Imagine a great college football player making the big leap to the professional ranks. Faced with the new requirements of competition at this level, he falls into the middle of the pack—he's no longer a superstar. Does he lose respect from others? No. He might lose superstar status, but no one disrespects, for example, Doug Flutie—a legendary college player who struggled to achieve greatness in the NFL.

In much the same way, marriage throws entirely new challenges at us. While I hope to be great at the game of marriage, I hope my wife respects the fact that a shared life is much more demanding—and richly textured!—than a single life. It might take years to master the intricacies. I'm not less of a man than I was before I said "I do." I am more tested.

In a similar way, a woman might be an accomplished pianist —the best in town. But at an international competition, she's judged as "fine but not extraordinary." Does that cause her to lose status in my eyes? Of course not. She simply walked into a forest with higher trees. I respect her for trying.

Perhaps that is the thing that causes disrespect most often —someone quits trying. I know of marriages where one party has said, "Enough. I'm done trying. I'm done disappointing and being disappointed." Whether that person leaves the marriage or withdraws and withholds emotionally, this is the ultimate show of disrespect. "I'm done with you. You're not worth it. We're not worth it." And for the other, this can trigger a profound loss of respect coupled with a varied set of responses—from desperate pursuit to desperate defeat.

STOP, TALK AND LISTEN

1. What about the garden image—are you okay if your partner grows? Why? Why not?
2. Why is adulthood tougher than earlier seasons?
3. If marriage is such a stretch, why bother? Is there enough compensation for the trouble? Like what?

The Maintenance Factor

Here's a potential problem: as I've already written, men tend to measure "the best" relationships according to the *low maintenance factor*. In other words, men would usually describe their best friendships as "the ones where I'm accepted for who I am; the ones that I don't have to measure or manipulate; the ones that I can walk away from for a year, and then just pick up where I left off; the ones that don't drain me." In other words, men tend to appreciate high-yield, low-cost relationships. The friendships that fall away are the ones that seem to require extraordinary investment.

The problem, of course, is that marriage requires steady maintenance, extraordinary investment and keen attention. Intimacy with a woman requires it, since she usually has a much more sophisticated dashboard of gauges and signals, and a much higher commitment to high-cost relational investment. Unlike most men, woman-to-woman relationships that are characterized by inattention usually fall away. Marriage relationships marked by inattention cool off, quickly and badly.

There are exceptions. Sometimes these needs and propensities are reversed. Sometimes both partners are high-maintenance relaters. In some cases, both are fine with an easy-going, steady-as-it-grows marriage.

But as I deal with couples before, during and after marriage, I tend to hear frustration from a woman whose husband "never shows up for our relationship" and from a man whose wife "just can't let our relationship be what it is." The outcome is usually subtle disrespect coupled with passive-aggression. He stops bringing his "A-game"—caring *attention*. She so often stops bringing the "X-game"—*sexual* attention. Cool becomes cold.

So keep trying. Don't give up. Men, never let things *just be*. Women, sometimes he'll respond better if you *just let him be*. Respect the fact that God made you different—one with a voracious commitment to growing closer and stronger, and the other with a tenacious capacity for accepting what is.

STOP, TALK AND LISTEN

1. Does this friendship stereotype fit you? If not, talk about what is.
2. Do either of you feel like all the maintenance is *on you*? What should you do?
3. Why do men tend to withhold "A" while women tend to withhold "X"?

Back to the Bible

The Bible teaches an outrageous commitment to mutual respect. The book of Philippians, chapter 2:3 puts it this way: "Consider others better than yourselves." It does not say that the other *is* more important, but it challenges each of us to put on this attitude. The book of Philippians then points to Jesus

respect

147

as the model of this attitude when he *emptied himself* of heavenly status and came to earth as a servant. Ephesians 5:21 teaches much the same thing: "Submit to one another out of reverence for Christ." The passage then urges wives to actually submit and to treat their husbands with utter respect. And it challenges men to *lay down their lives* for their wives, showing love and respect for her as if she were part of his own body.

One popular marriage curriculum [30] suggests that the one thing that men long for above all else from their wives is respect; the one thing women hunger for most is adoration. Ephesians 5:22-33 and 1 Peter 3:1-7 are the primary biblical texts that point to this. The author of the curriculum writes, "Five out of ten marriages today are ending in divorce because love alone is not enough. Yes, love is vital, especially for the wife, but what we've missed is the husband's need for respect."

Of course, men also need adoration and women also need respect. But if Emerson Eggerichs's observations are accurate at all, then women must fight the current of culture that teaches women to disrespect a man as a moderately-necessary-but-altogether-incurable-ignoramus.

And men must swim against the flow of a culture that makes exotic physical beauty the prerequisite for adoration. Men, if you revere Jesus, adore your wife. And let your adoration be laced with real respect for her entire personhood, not only her physical beauty.

Women, if you revere Jesus, respect your husband. And let your respect be laced with adoration—real affection.

"I remember how she used to look at me," he says. "And I remember when she quit looking at me that way. Now you'd think I shot her dog or something."

30 Emerson E. Eggerichs, *Love & Respect: The Love She Most Desires; The Respect He Desperately Needs* (Nashville: Thomas Nelson), 2004.

"Well, I remember," she says, "how he used to look at me; as if the sun rose and set in my eyes. He was curious, attentive, involved. He really seemed interested in me."

Don't let this happen. You can dig out of a hole like this with help, but it's better to stay out of it.

STOP, TALK AND LISTEN

1. Do you truly believe that the other person is as important as you are?
2. Are you willing to embrace the attitude that the other is *more* important?
3. Have you had *cool* seasons yet? How did you shake loose and heat it up?

"What Ifs" and "What Abouts"

What if I really have lost respect? What if my partner has made a succession of bad decisions and, frankly, proven to be a bad egg?

Get help together. Go on a journey with your partner (if he/she allows it) to discover where the train got off the track, and how to get back on track. You might uncover shame and real regret. Hopefully, you'll also discover humility and teachability. Don't give up!

If your partner won't work with you, pray like crazy. I've seen so many people face issues and truly transform in dramatic ways when loved ones have prayed diligently.

In extreme cases, intervention by a cadre of family and friends can shake someone out of self-destructive patterns and

respect

pave the way toward real help. A counselor can help with the how-to of intervention.

As for you, please learn to respect the fact that the best people have bad seasons. It could be you tomorrow.

I don't respect myself enough to marry a nice person. I choose mean, even abusive, people. Why, and what do I do now?

Why? That's a complex question. You might have watched a parent choose a troubled partner, and you think that's how it's supposed to be. You might enjoy *being* the sane, normal and even messianic partner. It's part of who you like to be—the island of calm in a stormy sea. Or perhaps you really are punishing yourself by choosing a barbarian. To varying degrees, all three reasons have their dangers.

Do the hard work. Find out why you're such a glutton for punishment. Then do more hard work—negotiate with your partner for a new way of being. If abuse continues, get help. If you're not married yet, get out today. This person is not for you.

My spouse quit trying. What do I do? I feel abandoned.

Some people believe that the marriage is actually over when one partner gives up. Some say that such an occurrence is even grounds for divorce in the Christian system—a kind of infidelity in that it is a betrayal in the deepest sense. I think that opinion is pushing it. It's sort of like giving up on a comatose patient when there's still brain activity.

With sympathy for how difficult it must be, I believe that those marriages represent the opportunity to grow deeper and stronger in patience and long-suffering. Loving well, even when others don't love us back, is part of life's curriculum. Some people are saddled with upper-division coursework. God be with you. Pass the test. Make the grade. Be an extraordinary, courageous partner.

CHAPTER 14

forgiveness

For what you've done or haven't done;
for all you might do or forget to do;
I will learn not to punish you
or to enslave our affections in chains of resentment.
Today I choose grace.

We hurt each other. This is a fact of life that's been happening for a long, long time. Sometimes we cause bruises and abrasions that heal with time and a modicum of care. At other times we assault each other, inflicting deep pain and profound harm. If there are couples reading this book who've somehow avoided the mutual infliction of pain, you are in a small minority—very small.

So forgiveness becomes absolutely critical in order for happiness to have any chance at all. People who can't or won't forgive do very badly in marriage. If we refuse to forgive and insist on stockpiling grievances, stewing over wrongs suffered and punishing the wrongdoer, we are placing a curse on our lives and a cloud over our own homes that nothing but true forgiveness can chase away.

STOP, TALK AND LISTEN

1. Are you a forgiving person? Why? Why not?
2. Can you think of someone that you hold a grudge toward? Why hasn't it been forgiven and resolved?

Why Is Forgiveness So Hard?

First, forgiveness is difficult because healing takes time. It's difficult to forgive quickly or completely when some emotional wounds take a long time to heal. While forgiving someone is an act of the will, healing is often beyond our control. We can put ourselves in healing environments or invite able healers to assist the process, but healing seems to have a time frame that's somewhat independent from forgiveness. Forgiveness itself can contribute to healing, since our insistence on punishing others is the equivalent of rubbing sandpaper on an abrasion. And healing helps forgiveness, since it's easier to forgive if a wound is not gaping and oozing. Still, the separate tracks of healing and forgiveness can make forgiveness tougher.

STOP, TALK AND LISTEN

1. Are you living with any gaping wounds? Are you still bleeding from some profound hurt from your past?
2. Is there a healed wound that flares up because you're holding a grudge? In other words, it's fine, except when you contemplate your revenge or indulge in ill-wishing?

How We Justify Bitterness

Second, forgiveness is difficult because we're capable of justifying our resentment with a host of objections.

"He isn't sorry enough. When he's really, *really* sorry, I might forgive."

"She's just going to do it to me again if I let her off this time."

"He'll think that I wasn't hurt that badly if I forgive. He needs to understand!"

When we say or think things like this, we refuse to offer the one thing that will open the door to resolution and promote the health of both partners. And our rationale is tainted by anger and pride.

No, he might not be sorry enough. He might not completely understand. But that's part of what is being forgiven. Even ignorance is forgivable.

And yes, she might do the same thing again, whether I forgive or not. But each offense needs to be processed individually, or else I'll face a huge debris field of bitterness that is almost impossible to clear away.

STOP, TALK AND LISTEN

1. What is your favorite justification for staying mad?
2. What kind of thinking helps you to break through objections and finally forgive?

Pride Cometh Before the Grudge

Third, forgiveness is elusive because we're reticent about admitting our own contributions to the conflict that left us smarting.

For example, it took a long time for me to address the deeper reasons behind my own igniting behaviors that, in part, contributed to my wife's rages. She takes complete responsibility for her anger management issues, but I am wholly responsible for my own bad behaviors and contributions to the health or unhealth of our relationship. It took plenty of soul-searching to see where I was broken and how my brokenness added to *our* vulnerability.

Examples: I was conflict-averse, so I didn't allow her to have ordinary mood swings without bugging her ("What's wrong? *What's wrong!*"). I was insecure, so I didn't like her to be annoyed with me ("What did I do? Why are *you* so bugged?"). I was smug about my rational ability to control my temper most of the time ("Why are *you* so angry? Can't we just talk?"). And while I forgave my wife quickly for her rages, however hurtful, I nursed a subtle attitude of victimization that on further examination was actually pride. As a whole, I'm not sure I was that easy to live with in those days. Yes, her rages needed healing and help. Part of the help came when I got honest with myself.

All to say, real forgiveness requires a more penetrating gaze into the mirror and the humility to own and address our own foibles.

STOP, TALK AND LISTEN

1. Do you tend to blame a lot, or are you more prone toward owning responsibility and doing personal inventories?
2. Now tell the truth about how you perceive your partner's self-examination. Ouch! Careful.

We Forgive as We Are Forgiven

Finally, forgiveness is tough to give when we ignore or devalue the forgiveness offered to us by God. Jesus tells the story of the unmerciful servant,[31] a man who is forgiven an enormous debt and then turns around and squeezes another man who owes him a small debt. This sad picture of blind resentment is true about every one of us when we refuse to forgive.

Jesus even suggests that if we don't forgive, God won't forgive us. In my opinion, Jesus is saying that if we don't forgive others, then we must not believe in God's forgiveness of us. Therefore, without believing in God's forgiveness, we will miss the benefits of it altogether. If we do believe in God's forgiveness, we'll be swept up in the spirit and current of God's grace: having been forgiven much, I forgive much.

This points to a deeper issue that could underlie almost every failure to forgive. We don't forgive ourselves because we can't imagine how God could forgive us. And because we can't stop

---

31 Matthew 18:21-35.

punishing ourselves, we continue to imagine that God wants to punish us. And because we deserve to be punished, so do others. In short, the people who are hardest on others are usually pretty hard on themselves as well. When this is true, the whole conduit of love, grace and mercy is clogged up. We have a faulty image of God, a shameful notion of ourselves and a punishing spirit toward others. This adds up to a very sad life. That sadness results in marriages burdened by bitterness.

The bitterness of unforgiveness, says a friend of mine, is like swallowing rat poison and waiting for the rat to die. Bitterness is toxic. I believe that medical science will one day prove a correlation between some cancers and an unforgiving spirit.

STOP, TALK AND LISTEN

1. Do you believe in God's forgiveness, or do you see God as a punishing dictator?
2. Have you forgiven yourself for your mistakes and weaknesses, or do you tend to live with a lot of shame and regret?
3. When you are tough on yourself, do you catch yourself being tough on others?

So How Do We Actually Forgive?

The critical first step is to pray to God, with humility, for forgiveness of our own wrongdoings. The Bible says that "If we confess our sins, he is faithful and just and will forgive us our sins and purify us from all unrighteousness."[32] This first exercise in self-cleansing opens the floodgates for mercy and grace to flow into us and then through us. To be effective, we need to believe in the forgiving nature of God and then offer a kind of absolution. "I am forgiven."

---

32 1 John 1:9.

The second step of forgiveness is to pray for the capacity to forgive. That gift will not be withheld by a loving Father. Jesus tells us to pray for those who persecute us, and even to love our enemies. God is not in the grudge-keeping business, so don't think that he's participating in your refusals to forgive. Pray for capacity and pray for your spouse. Like *The Grinch who Stole Christmas,* your heart will actually grow at least two sizes.

The third step is to evaluate with prayer, and even with a thoughtful helper, why the actions of the other person have been so hurtful. It's possible that we were vulnerable or overly sensitive because of some previous experience. It might even be possible that the other person hurt us by exposing our *true self* in ways that we're trying desperately to cover up or deny. Sometimes we're deeply hurt because we feel profoundly misunderstood or disrespected. In the worst cases, we've been abandoned, abused or betrayed. Those "big three" hurts inflict the deepest wounds. Whatever lies underneath the pain, understanding will help forgiveness to be authentic.

When possible, forgiveness is then facilitated by direct conversation. In some relationships, this isn't possible. We might be forgiving someone from the past, or from a distance, or even someone who's dead. But in marriage, we've got to talk! Communication means understanding. Understanding leads to acceptance, respect, intimacy and real resolution.

STOP, TALK AND LISTEN

1. Have you, or have you often, appealed to God for forgiveness? Why is or isn't that part of your life?
2. Do you pray for the expansion and softening (even strengthening) of your own heart?
3. When you hold a grudge, what's at the heart of it?

But Don't I Deserve an Apology?

Of course, it helps when the offending partner fully apologizes and owns up to his/her part in the mess. But even if your partner is blind or stubborn about sharing responsibility, there is still the possibility of forgiveness. In fact, you might be forgiving his or her very blindness and stubbornness!

I once heard a story told about Napoleon as he prepared to punish a young man for desertion. The man's mother intervened, begging for mercy.

"He doesn't deserve mercy," said Napoleon.

"If he deserved it," replied the mother, "it wouldn't be mercy."

From this story we learn that forgiveness is an act of mercy —undeserved favor. Real grace means a sustained propensity for offering unearned pardons.

A lifestyle of forgiveness is called "grace." Gracious people are much more skilled and equipped for marriage. Forgiveness is readily at hand. Forgiveness is swift and complete. Forgiveness is often rendered in the instant of offense, and bitterness never gets the tiniest foothold. Grace is a predisposition toward the whole world that says, "I already forgive you for whatever you're about to do to me." Informed and infused by God's grace, we consistently give grace to others.

STOP, TALK AND LISTEN

1. Do you tend to withhold forgiveness until an apology is offered? Why?
2. Are you a gracious person? How so?
3. Do you tend to punish, or are you someone who leaves that to God's discernment?
4. Have you been hurt enough that your bigger problem is trusting more than forgiving?

forgiveness

Don't Pull the Eject Lever; Unless ...

My concern is that some people are quick to pull out of a relationship. With claims of emotional abuse, some are actually refusing to forgive fairly ordinary human behavior. Some people pull away from marriage based on a carefully crafted case of being "wronged." Slights and insensitivities and insults that most other people would excuse or forgive are viewed as capital crimes. In other words, some people are looking for a perfect spouse ... and that person simply doesn't exist. Or else the "offended party" is allergic to the hard work involved in creating and maintaining intimacy. Part of that hard work is forgiveness and reconciliation.

If you are on the verge of marrying someone who is, by nature and practice, highly critical and woefully unforgiving, *stop*. Don't do it. Find the courage to flee that relationship. Forgive the person, but break off the engagement. If you don't, you are walking eyes-wide-open into a demoralizing experience.

If *you* are that unforgiving person, do yourself and your intended spouse a huge favor. Put the wedding on hold. Pursue the best counselor you can find at any cost. Heal, change and grow. Then present yourself for marriage.

I offer similar advice if you are on the verge of marriage and one person is verbally abusive. Stop the madness. Postpone the wedding. Get help. Change. Grow. Then, perhaps, you will have enough health to create a foundation that can be built on. Forgiveness is a great thing, but don't walk into a marriage that will obviously test forgiveness to its very limits. If the abuse is physical, get out. Cancel the wedding. If your relationship *ever* has a future, your partner must absolutely prove that healing and change is real.

Only once have I counseled a couple not to go through with their wedding. Every time this couple was in my office, they fought like wild animals. Their relational histories were not characterized by success. When I finally asked, "Why are you getting married?" they looked at me with wide eyes of naiveté. "We're in love."

I went through with the wedding, as a favor to the groom's mother. It was a farce. The marriage lasted less than a year. I regret participating.

Most of the time, couples present well in my office. They're eager to give marriage a real chance and are receptive to all of my counsel. But even then, marriage gets tough in seasons.

Forgive. Heal. Learn.

Forgive again.

STOP, TALK AND LISTEN

1. If you had to cut and run before marriage, could you?
2. Are there a significant number of moments when you wonder if you should go through with the wedding? Why? How are you processing your doubts?

Is There Ever a Time to Refuse Forgiveness?

Whenever we refuse to forgive, we harm ourselves and others. Even in cases of terrible abuse, abandonment or betrayal, our souls find healing when we find the grace to forgive. Not that we excuse awful behavior, or subject ourselves to terrible offenses in an ongoing way. Sometimes trust is irretrievable and ongoing relationship simply isn't possible. Still, we must learn to forgive.

Of course, that extraordinary level of forgiveness requires help from God and a generous application of empathy. People who abuse, abandon and betray are (like all of us) broken and weak. That acknowledgement helps us work through the anger

forgiveness

and disappointment as we gradually release the need to punish offenders. Our wrath gives way to pity, and finally to a genuine hope that everyone involved can one day be healed and on a good footing again. We lose the limp of victimization and go forward into a new future.

Now, let's face it. Neither of you is likely to behave monstrously. So get ready for a steady diet of abrasions and bumps and irritations. And get ready to forgive often and completely.

Everyone has an opinion about the *one big issue* that most often leads to divorce. Here is mine: a refusal to forgive. In my opinion, bitterness is the number one cause of divorce. So please, choose the high road, which is grace and forgiveness.

STOP, TALK AND LISTEN

1. Have you ever had to forgive a monster? How did it go? What did it take? If you can't, why not?

"What Ifs" and "What Abouts"

But what if I get hurt again?
You will. Did you really think marriage would be painless?

But what if he doesn't change?
If he does, it'll be slow progress. So don't hold your breath. Forgive.

But what if she doesn't apologize?
Maybe she just can't see clearly yet. Are you going to keep punishing her for that deficit?

Ultimately, that's what forgiveness is—the decision to stop punishing someone, actually or internally, for a wrong suffered. Whenever we withhold affection or fellowship or the benefits of a friendly nature, we are punishing the other person. The longer we withhold, the more we become the harm doers in need of forgiveness.

But what if I don't trust him? He's hurt me before and he'll hurt me again. Am I supposed to expose myself again and again to his assaults? That depends on the nature of the "assaults." If you're actually being abused, physically or verbally, you need to get out to a safe place. Caring helpers will assist as you discern the steps for building a future with or without your abusive spouse. Some abusive people get help, heal and live peaceable lives. Others can't or won't.

If the "assault" is something less than actual abuse, simply communicate your fear and find ways to partner together to rebuild trust. Use a skilled counselor. There's no shame in seeking a pastor, therapist or trusted friend to moderate and guide conversations.

My spouse is so easily bent out of shape. I find myself apologizing for breathing! What do I do?
First, do the hard work of mirror time. Are you abrasive and injurious in your manner? Is there some legitimacy to the grievances? If so, start some programmed change.

Second, tell your partner how you feel. "I feel as if I'm constantly failing you. If I am, then we need to really talk. If I'm not, then I need to ask for some change in how we interact."

My spouse is a list keeper. When we argue, all the old grievances come popping back out. I'm told that I'm forgiven, but with the slightest provocation it becomes apparent that I'm not.
It's possible that you really have been forgiven. But when something happens that picks an old scab, the bleeding starts

all over again. So does the forgiveness process. With some injuries, we have to forgive several times before it's actually gone from our lives.

I hurt my spouse. Forgiveness seems to be a long way off. What do I do? Wait. Pray. Give. Serve. Earn trust one day at a time. Ask, periodically, if there's anything you can do to foster the process—but don't be a pest.

If it still doesn't happen, ask for the help of a third party.

CHAPTER 15

friendship

Perhaps we could pull this off without friendship.
Others have.
But why?

Now we get to the fun part. Friendship is a critical *building block* of a strong marriage. It usually takes couples awhile to mention it on their lists because they're afraid it sounds frivolous. But it's not frivolous. Friendship makes a huge difference in a relationship.

Why?

Friendship is important because it was probably one of the early features of the relationship that brought you together. Yes, there were other attractions. But this relationship elevated to a new level because, at least in part, your friendship grew naturally. Needless to say, we want to preserve and grow all of the elements of attraction that brought us together, rather than carelessly neglecting or misplacing them.

Friendship is also fun! Life is heavy enough already. We don't need a marriage that feels like a bag of rocks. Friendship lifts our spirits. Friendship lightens the load. Friendship means companionship—someone to laugh with, cry with, groan with, tease with and adventure with. Every sunset is prettier if you have someone next to you to point with and exclaim to: "Wow! Look at those colors!"

And friendship is smart. As the Bible says, "Two are better than one because they have a good return for their work. If one falls down, his friend can help him up. But pity the man who falls and has no one to help him up!"[33] Life works better with friends. A spouse is a friend for life.

STOP, TALK AND LISTEN

1. How did your friendship first develop? What brought you together other than physical attraction?
2. What are some things you do together that you can't imagine doing alone?
3. Describe the things that feed your other friendships. What do you do with your friends?
4. In building friendships, are you typical regarding female "face time" and male "side-by-side" experiences? If you are different, how so?

Other Friends

It's also important to let this friendship be what it is, without loading it up with expectation. While your marriage will likely be your closest friendship in many ways, other friends are necessary to offer elements of companionship that can't be gleaned from your marriage.

For example, my wife knows that I like a good debate over issues and world events. While she's actually very informed, she tends to suffer under the tension of debate. Occasionally she's apologized for "not being what I need." My quick response? "I have other friends for that. You don't have to be everything for me."

---

33 Ecclesiastes 4:9-10.

Meanwhile, my wife loves to spar and tease and jab. She grew up among brothers and relates well with the language of sparring. Unfortunately, I'm rather earnest in relationships and not always good at sparring and teasing. My wife needs other friends—sometimes *my* friends—to swap punches with. This is great! My friends like it, and I do too, knowing that I can't be everything for her.

Obviously, we all have to be careful with other-gender friendships. But as trust grows and as we learn to cherish our marriages *for what they are,* we feel more freedom to find elements of friendship in others. While my wife is, by far, my best friend, she's not my only friend. And I'm not her only friend.

What about confidential friendships and intimate information sharing? Am I threatened if my wife has deep conversations with people other than me? And what if I'm the topic of conversation?

I recommend that intimate friends be *cleared* with your spouse, as I mentioned in chapter 6. In other words, my wife has friends that I feel safe with. They handle secrets well. Even though they sympathize with my wife like every good female friend, they also encourage my wife to respect me and forgive me when I blow it.

She has had other friends that, frankly, scare the daylights out of me! Given the chance, they would blab our private information to others. Or they would coach my wife to be embittered toward me—even to leave me!

All this to say, I care about my wife's friendships and she cares about mine. She doesn't want me with a friend who's going to drag me to strip clubs or coax me toward shady adventures that threaten the sanctity of marriage. Honestly, let's be smart about the people we befriend!

Still, we need other friends. Even deep friends.

STOP, TALK AND LISTEN

1. When marriage comes, other friendships change. Tell each other which friendships you'd like to keep investing in.
2. Are there any friendships that seem to interfere with *your* friendship? What are you willing to do about that?
3. Ask each other, "Do you feel safe with my friends, or are you afraid that I might share too much?"

The Makings of Marital Friendship

Depth aside, most friendships flourish with laughter and play. Most couples laugh a lot when they're courting. Play is the primary stuff of dating. So then, when bills and jobs and fatigue and kids and overgrown lawns and dirty toilets and a host of other demands set in, play gets pushed into a corner. Sometimes couples stop playing together.

Do everything you can to ensure that this doesn't happen! Go on dates. Watch your favorite show. Play your favorite game. Read the funnies together. Have *funny sex* every now and then (it doesn't always have to be serious or romantic). Go on walks. Go to the beach. Shoot baskets. Play tennis. Turn on the music and dance. Get in a tickle fight. Cultivate friendship with that fun couple next door or down the street; the ones who make you laugh.

While most pastors will tell you, "the family that prays together stays together," I'm here to tell you—the family that *plays* together stays together, too.

STOP, TALK AND LISTEN

1. What are the things that make you really laugh together?
2. Did you watch your parents play? How does their marriage influence you?

unshakable

Showing Up for Each Other

Friendship also involves showing up in crisis. All of us, especially men, need to learn how to be sympathetic listeners. As I mentioned in previous chapters, it's not uncommon for women to need lamentation as a process of expressing and sifting through hurts and frustrations. Since most men internalize such things, we aren't adept at listening. It's quite common for men to be impatient with this process and to try to fix problems with advice or conclusive statements. Men even tend to minimize or rationalize—"She isn't trying to hurt you. She's just...."

"Are you on *her* side?"

"No, I'm just trying to...."

"Why do you always take the other person's side? Can't you be on my side for once?"

"Why do I have to choose sides? I'm just trying to ..." rationalize. And what she needs is someone to sympathize.

Women, you need to know that men rarely sympathize with each other. Reiterating from chapter 2, when men share problems, we problem-solve, rationalize, explain away or other-wise minimize emotion. In other words, your husband will be a novice in the art of sympathetic listening. You must prepare for and accept this even as you coach him in this new life skill. Men, we must learn to count to ten thousand before we offer a single word of advice. She isn't asking you to fix the problem or to fix her. She's asking you to listen and to actually care how she feels—even if her feelings seem irrational to you.

Realize that a number of couples will experience a role reversal. Since a smaller percentage of women are more rational than emotional, and since a smaller percentage of men are more emotional than rational (see chapter 12) some couples will need to flip-flop as they read this. Male or female "thinkers" tend to marry "feelers," so the thinking partner will need to learn how to do active, sympathetic listening, while the "feeler" processes and filters emotional reactions.

Another way to view this, gender aside, is to say that some people are internal processors and others are external. Internal processors generally won't communicate feelings until they are pretty much resolved. External processors put it all on the table for sifting and sorting. If you are married to an external processor, your job is mostly to care, not to abbreviate the process by intervening.

The sooner we accept these differences, the better. In my opinion, marriages suffered immensely during the few decades that our culture pretended that there is no difference between most men and most women. While that season of denial made sense during a time when every sensible person fought for women's rights and equality among genders, it now makes sense to tell the obvious truth—men and women are equal but not the same.

STOP, TALK AND LISTEN

1. Finish the sentence: I feel understood when _____
   _____.

2. When I'm down and you _____,
   it helps me feel better.

How Interesting!

Friendship also means showing interest in the other person. I love basketball. It isn't necessary for my wife to play basketball, but it would harm our friendship if she had no interest in *my* basketball experiences. My wife is an avid treasure hunter (that's *code* for bargain shopper). I'm not. But if I show little interest in her passions and hobbies, I'm starving the friendship.

Sometimes, your partner's interests and hobbies might frustrate you because they seem to steal time and passion that could otherwise belong to you. Communicate your feelings with "I" language: "I'm glad you love to play golf. But sometimes I feel left behind when I'm home alone for hours at a time." Negotiate. Find a way to make it work for both of you. And don't let resentment build up to the point where you begin to *hate* your partner's hobbies.

STOP, TALK AND LISTEN

1. Talk about hobbies and interests. Do you feel supported in yours?

One Final Observation

Some people cherish most the relationships that require the least maintenance. Ask the question, "Am I a high-maintenance friend?" Anything close to a "yes" in response should cause me to ask whether I'm demanding too much from this friendship or relying too much on this friendship to make me happy and whole. There are other friendships, especially with God, that lead to real contentment.

Les and Leslie Parrott[34] describe the "A-frame" marriage as codependent—two unhealthy people leaning too heavily on each other. They describe the "H-frame" marriage as two independent people barely connected at all. The healthiest relationship is the "M-frame"—two healthy, interdependent people who share life connected and side by side in a way that really amounts to health. They can stand alone, but prefer to experience life together.

---

34 Les and Leslie Parrott, *Saving Your Marriage Before It Starts: Seven Questions to Ask Before and After You Marry* (Grand Rapids: Zondervan), 2006.

"What Ifs" and "What Abouts"

But we really don't laugh or play or interact that much. Our thing is lovemaking. We're connected at the hip—literally. Isn't that enough?

I'll never say never; but it's not likely to be enough. Of course, there might be a couple somewhere that endures each other or nominally coexists apart from sex, while sex works its magic. It's more likely that sex won't be enough.

We really are like a dog and a cat. Our whole view of interrelating is different. We're making it work, but it is hard work.

If you're engaged, you should really be asking, "Is it supposed to be this hard?" In a sense, it's good that you're already addressing the tougher aspects of relationship; but in another sense, make sure that you are honest about the fit of your coming marriage. Engagement is a testing time, and not only the time to plan the wedding.

If you're married, welcome to reality. Keep going. Make it work.

We have such different hobbies. Can this be a good thing?

Of course! Those other experiences and relationships can make life full and complete. Just keep the curiosity alive. Don't shut yourself or your partner out of each others' lives. The time apart can be good for you, but don't create completely separate lives.

CHAPTER 16

faith

*When we pursue God first and most,
our love will grow more and better.*

If it seems like an afterthought this late in the book, it is. Not for me. I would have placed this core value of faith in the first few chapters. But for most couples, even ardent Christians, the word "faith" pops up as an "Oh, yeah. We need to add faith." Or God. Or spirituality. Or church.

Why so late? You'd think that couples would say it early at least to impress the pastor. After all, this is the first exercise that I do with couples, and they are still self-conscious about proving themselves to me with "the right answers." So why is faith in chapter sixteen?

This Is Not Easy

The most obvious answer is that very few couples have developed a strategy for integrating faith with marriage. And while each partner might have an intentional and applied personal spirituality, seeking God together is not an easy prospect. Add to that the likelihood that neither partner grew up watching Mom and Dad integrate faith into marriage successfully, and you can understand why faith tends to be an afterthought.

After twenty-five years, my wife and I still strain to groove any consistent family devotional time. My wife, frankly, is much better at routines and rituals that bring faith into the home. I'm

faith

better at spontaneous outbursts of spiritual awareness. My wife reads a type of devotional guide that I have difficulty enjoying, and the books I read don't generally engage my wife. I feel closest to God when I'm writing, speaking and serving hordes of people at church. She feels closest to God when she's with a close friend, creating beauty, serving her family or alone in a crowd. All to say that we have different devotional patterns. It's fine that they are parallel and not always intersecting—but sometimes we want more than fine.

STOP, TALK AND LISTEN

1. Talk together about faith in your home growing up. How did it find expression?
2. What are the aspects of faith that find their way into your relationship now?

Talking with God

Praying together has been an intimate and satisfying part of our marriage. We haven't done it as often as most people would assume. Some of the sweetest times, though, have been spontaneous. One or the other of us has simply prompted a time of prayer for the other, or for one of our children, or for the vacation we are about to embark on, or for some difficult meeting or encounter that's pending. Part of the sweetness has been the spontaneity and periodic nature of these prayer moments. Part of the loss is that we haven't done it more. I encourage you to try it.

Men, before you go out the door one morning, simply pull your wife close and whisper into her ear a prayer for her day—simple, short, honest. It will bless her. You will touch her deeply. Wives, you can do the same for your husbands.

Yes, we pray together before every meal. Even in restaurants. I take my wife's hand and initiate a brief, open-eyed prayer. It's intimate to look into her eyes while we pray, and it doesn't feel as if we're bowing our heads for prayer "in order to be seen by others," which Jesus warns against. I grab her hand, look into her eyes, and say something like, "Thanks, Lord, for my friend, for my food and for the privilege of being right here, right now."

STOP, TALK AND LISTEN

1. Try a prayer right now, something simple like, "Lord, I thank you for _____."
2. What makes this difficult for some couples?

Men, Listen Up

Men, most women like it when we initiate these moments. Even though our wives' prayer lives might be more developed than ours, this is one area where most women hope that we'll take the lead. This is true in part because women don't like the feeling that they're mothering us. "George, have you said your prayers yet? Now go brush your teeth!" It's also true because these women who love us are concerned about us. They see how we compartmentalize our lives and they know how easily God's piece gets squeezed out. So it thrills our wives to hear us pray and it touches them deeply when we lead.

The abuse of that leadership kills the faith element of some marriages. Weird concepts of male leadership create lasting pain in some households. Some men say stupid things to their wives like, "The Bible says that I'm the head of this household and that you're supposed to submit to me. So do what I say, woman!" That's an awful abuse of scripture.

Sorry. I don't mean to judge. But that's not what the Bible teaches, and every time the Bible is misrepresented in that way, hundreds of God-curious people run away screaming into the night. Jesus himself has an obvious allergy regarding bad religion. The worst kinds of religion teach power mongering.

faith

STOP, TALK AND LISTEN

1. Why do men have difficulty initiating spiritual things?
2. Who tends to be the initiator in your relationship?
3. How do you both feel about that?

What Does the Bible Say?

Various passages in the Bible speak briefly about marriage. As I mentioned regarding compromise, the most thorough New Testament section on marriage is in the fifth chapter of Ephesians. The Apostle Paul is instructing the church in how to approach vital relationships—humbly and with a heart of submission and service. In the midst of that conversation, he brings up marriage as an ultimate example of these principles. In fact, he suggests that marriage is actually a parable of sorts—a symbolic reminder of the relationship between Jesus and the church.

Most people begin reading at chapter 5, verse 22. "Wives, submit [or be subject] to your husbands as to the Lord. For the husband is the head of the wife as Christ is the head of the church." Women in the first century would not have been surprised by those words. Male dominance and female subservience were the norm. Paul was teaching women to do something they'd seen their mothers do—submit—but to actually do it for good reason: respect and love.

The male reader or listener in the first century probably nodded his head and began to settle more deeply into a sense of his own supremacy. At least until the reading continued. "Husbands, love your wives just as Christ loved the church and gave himself up for her." In other words: Men, you want to lead? You want to be the big shot? You want to be the Jesus-figure in the home?

Fine. Do it. Lead in the way Jesus led. Lay down your life. Let go of your grasp on the need for self-importance and control. Come to serve, not to be served. Nurture. Teach. Heal.

Shepherd. Care. Listen. Touch. Rescue. Bless. Cherish. Sacrifice. Die to yourself and follow Jesus. He loved his bride (the Church) by dying for her. As for obedience, he simply said, "If you love me you'll obey me."

If we ever get to the point where we have to play the "obey me and submit to me" card, we've already blown it. Do you see that women who really love their husbands are happy to honor a healthy, Christlike brand of headship? But if we get bossy and self-important and have to throw around a funky twist on male authority, we've missed the whole thing.

STOP, TALK AND LISTEN

1. Do you like the word "submit"? Why? Why not?
2. What do you know about Jesus' approach to leadership?

Submit to One Another

The truth about the Ephesians 5 teaching is that it starts in verse 21, not verse 22. Sadly, most modern versions of the Bible stick a heading and a space between those verses as if they were disconnected thoughts. They so completely are not! "Submit to one another out of reverence for Christ. Wives, submit to your husbands ... husbands love your wives by giving yourself up for her." The message is not old-fashioned male dominance; rather, it's newfangled mutual love and respect. Servanthood. Other-centeredness.

"Consider others better than yourselves," writes Paul.[35] It doesn't say the other person *is* more important, but the message is to put on the attitude of Christ and *consider* the other person before yourself.

How does this play out?

My slowly-learned-lesson is that showing respect for my wife is far more important than having things *my way*. When

---

35 Philippians 2:3.

I get *my way,* I'm winning a battle while I lose the war. When I get *my way,* I'm gaining three yards in a cloud of dust, only to be penalized fifteen yards for a personal foul—roughing. I'm even harming my own soul.

Behaving as if I'm God is actually the antithesis of how God reveals himself through Jesus. God's profound respect for the dignity of our free will is at the heart of an authentic relationship with God. Our respect for the free will of others is at the heart of an authentic relationship with each other.

So in marriage, if my wife submits to me and serves me and obeys me because *she has to,* then I have a slave, not a wife. And I'll never know if she actually loves me or respects me. She might just be performing a duty, which sounds horrible to me. I'd much rather have a real relationship of actual love.

Not that love and servanthood is always easy. Sometimes it's costly and sacrificial, as it was for Jesus. And sometimes submission is pure hard work. Putting aside my need to be right or to be in control isn't always natural.

But with God's supernatural help, this is our life curriculum: to learn how to serve. This can be a steep learning curve if our motif for marriage has been steeped in another model.

STOP, TALK AND LISTEN

1. Do you ever feel bossed or enslaved in your relationship? Describe.
2. Are there times or areas of life when you have a hard time serving or submitting to the other?

Have We Gone Too Far?

Truthfully, in modern marriages, I see more subservient men and bossing women. The old joke among women used to be, "He might be the head, but I'm the neck that turns the head." These days, our television culture paints a picture of the husband as the lazy idiot and the wife as the frustrated, overworked, under-valued superhero. Long gone are the wise and good-humored Ward Cleaver images, replaced forever by the bungling Tim "the Tool Man" Taylor—or worse, Homer Simpson. In television marriages, the question seems to be, "How long can this smart, competent woman put up with the idiot she married?"

Part of the reason we laugh at the sitcom is that it mirrors many of the marriages we witness. It's common to see marriages where the man has abdicated any real leadership (servant leadership or any other type) and women are controlling and overtly disrespectful. The sad thing is that the couple finally comes for counseling when the man has acted out in passive-aggressive or active-aggressive ways.

I'm *not* blaming women for the bad behavior of men. I am suggesting that men often act like jerks when they're pushed into a corner, or when they feel utterly disrespected and disregarded.

Ultimately, this is not a male or female problem. Rather, it's the human problem. Out of our insecurity, we pursue power and control. Jesus taught and lived a better way. And Paul teaches a better way, using marriage as the emblem. Mutual submission is the way, marked by practiced respect and authentic regard for the other.

STOP, TALK AND LISTEN

1. How did your parents make decisions?
2. Do you want to do things in a similar way, or differently?

One Example of Mutual Submission

"What movie are we going to tonight?"

"What would you like to see?"

"No, you first. We went to my movie last time."

"Yes, but I chose the restaurant."

"I know, but I like to spoil you."

faith

"Thanks, but can I spoil you tonight?"

And so goes the mutually respectful, mutually submissive marriage. It involves partners putting their partners first. Eventually, they choose a movie. But both partners feel honored by the other.

"Oh barf!" says the cynic. And the cynic will be ten times more likely to clean up the barf in divorce court.

"But what about my hopes? What about me!"

Communicate your hopes, honestly and in a freehanded way. I'm not suggesting that anyone choke on personal wants or suck it up all the time. I'm only suggesting that the best marriages are characterized by the give-and-take of mutual respect. This is the best way and it's clearly, biblically, God's way.

STOP, TALK AND LISTEN

1. Can you think of a time when you've actually argued with each other over the privilege of being the giver instead of the receiver?
2. Are you cynical about whether mutual submission is possible for you?

Any Other Cues to Making Faith Part of Marriage?

1. Be an active part of a faith community where this approach to life is encouraged by a steady diet of teaching and experience.
2. Keep reading, learning and studying about God and God's life principles. If you don't study together, at least spur each other on.
3. Talk about God and your internal lives. This is intensely personal and every bit as helpful as sex in building intimacy —as long as one person isn't being shamed by the other. If you find yourself in a spiritually superior posture, please understand what a put-off that is. Again, respect the place of your partner on his or her spiritual journey.

4. Again, try praying together.
5. Practice, practice, practice being a servant. Treat your partner like royalty. Be your partner's loyal subject, "out of reverence for Christ."

Jesus said that in laying down our lives we actually find life. Marriage is the proving ground for that theory. After a quarter-century of struggling and practicing, my wife and I can tell you that this model is proving itself. We wish it on you.

"What Ifs" and "What Abouts"

What if my partner doesn't share my interest in faith matters?
This can be a more serious problem than most people realize. Faith (or nonfaith) is a deeply felt and central matter that shapes the entirety of our lives. It is usually foundational or causal in the formation of every other core value. It is also a sure footing that most of us fall back on when life gets slippery. If I fall back to faith and my partner falls back on something else, we could find ourselves in very different places during the slippery seasons.

It's also hard on the intimacy of a marriage when something as deeply felt as our faith is not one of the topics that we can share.

What does it mean when the Bible says not to be "unequally yoked"?[36]
Don't build critical partnerships with someone whose core values are intrinsically different than yours. In other words, that Bible verse is a premise of this book.

---

36 2 Corinthians 6:14.

But my partner supports my faith without practicing it!
Good. You're lucky. For now. Sorry, I'm sure your partner is wonderful. But it's difficult for a nonpracticing person to sustain support for the faith-practicing person. And this critical area *deserves* support.

As with couples who quit going to church, believing persons who marry nonbelievers so often slide away from the fervency of faith. There are so many exceptions, of course. But many, many people suffer this mismatch for the rest of their married lives. I counsel against it. Marriages that differ greatly in this area often survive, but are less likely to thrive.

But what if I'm already married to a person who doesn't practice my faith?
Make the best of it. Live your faith with as much energy and clarity as you can. Don't force faith on your partner, but make periodic invitations in openhanded ways.

Love and honor your spouse as Christ teaches us. Model submission as an outpouring of affection and respect. Pray for your spouse—forgiveness and reconciliation will help enormously. And keep the faith.

Keep going to church, even when it seems inconvenient. Isolated faith is a spiraling death march.

Most of all, keep going and growing. You'll have to be an initiator and caretaker of your growth, since your partner is unlikely to encourage this—and might even discourage it.

What if I'm the one without faith? How can I be supportive?
Encourage your partner to be loyal to faith matters. Negotiate ways to do this without being untrue to yourself. Ask questions about your partner's experiences and try to show genuine interest without judgment, just as you would hope for interest in matters critical to your personal wholeness.

CHAPTER 17

affection

Whatever I might feel,
I want to exercise the power of touch
and to give all you need to be sure of your value in my life.

Finally and sheepishly, most couples mention affection or sexuality or physical intimacy as a *building block*. One couple even blurted out "action!"

In most cases, I agree. It can be a core value, especially if we're honest. Many people would say that without sex, marriage is somewhat pointless. Without sex, some might say, "It would be easier to live with someone of my own gender." This is an understandable view.

The beauty of sexual affection is that it's geared up according to principles of mutuality and service—like the whole of marriage. The real turn-on of sex is turning on our partners. In the naked and vulnerable world of sexual give-and-take, we see a raw and powerful emblem for the entirety of marriage. We live and love to serve and please the other.

Oh, I know that it's both more and less than that. Sometimes sex is beautiful and other times it's funny. Sometimes we make love to bond and other times it helps us fall asleep. Sometimes it's experimental and *out there*. Other times it's familiar and comfortable. Sometimes it's loaded with emotion and other times it's pure animal behavior.

Again, though, so it is with marriage. Not always, but often, sexuality is a compass and a thermometer and a thermostat and an x-ray that both sets and measures the wellness of a marriage.

I say, *not always*. There are physical or emotional reasons why sex can be only a small part of the whole picture. Illness, depression and seasons of life can affect our ability to enjoy all aspects of sexuality. In those times, sexual things should *not* be viewed as a *building block*. Other *building blocks* are much more reliable and enduring and less subject to the coursing seasons of ever-changing lives.

STOP, TALK AND LISTEN

1. Without sex, would you get married? Why or why not?
2. If sexuality is a thermometer, what is your relational temperature?

This Is All God's Plan

God made us to be sexual beings and chose to make it a colorful, dynamic, evolving experience. Realize that God could easily have made procreation a utilitarian event—like flossing your teeth or taking out the garbage. Instead, God made this encounter lush with intrigue and monumentally enjoyable in the right context and in the hands of skilled participants.

As I mentioned in chapter 5, if you are already sexually active as a couple before marriage, I strongly encourage you to abstain until your wedding night. God intended sex for marriage as the ultimate binding element. One problem with premarital sex is that it creates a premature bond. Some couples get knitted together sexually and emotionally before it's time, and then stay together because they can't bear the thought of breaking up—even if their core values aren't aligned and their friendship is only moderately successful.

One benefit of abstaining for a season is practical. It gives you a chance to make sure that the binding force in your relationship is something better than sexual attraction, or even a kind of sexual addiction. Time spent sexually apart can lend some perspective while you evaluate other parts of the relationship.

Spiritually, many of us know when we've gone too far. A subtle shame can make us sheepish before God. Premarried couples are on the verge of this huge life decision and transition. Now is *not* the time to feel far from God. You need God and God needs you to go into marriage with a clear conscience and an active prayer life. Now isn't the time to be hiding from God.

So ask forgiveness for jumping the gun and establish a season of "second virginity." The couples I know who've decided to do this (even non-Christians) have thanked me profusely afterward for the excellent idea. They felt better about themselves, their decision to marry and their relationships with God.

One final benefit—the wedding night felt fresh and wonderful! For sexually active couples, the wedding night can feel like Christmas morning for the children who secretly peeked at all their presents before the big day. It's a definite joy stealer. So why not pause and wait. Let the wedding night be like the best Christmas you've ever experienced!

STOP, TALK AND LISTEN

1. How do you feel about your premarital sex life? Too much? Too little? Is there any shame before God? Talk to each other.
2. What would your ideal wedding night be like?

Practice, Practice, Practice

Back to sex itself. It's something we learn and practice. It's like going to school; but what a school! Figure out what works. Experiment. Know that it rarely works the way it appears in

affection

movies. Most of us feel clumsy; remember to laugh at yourself and not your partner. Remember to give your partner plenty of reassurance and direction and gratitude. Take turns. Give and take. Explore. Affirm. Shower the other person with affection. Use thoughtful words to describe the things that were and weren't satisfying. Don't assume!

Okay, now that our cheeks are red, let's ask why. Why? Because sex is so naked! It's an exercise in vulnerability and transparency. We bare our whole selves for the sake of intimacy and deep companionship, and then hope the other feels good about it. No, we hope the other feels *great!*

It's generous. It's risky. It's frisky! It's fun!

At least it can be. For some couples, sex becomes the first or worst battlefield. Please understand that God intended sexuality to be a bonding experience, not a relational wedge or weapon.

STOP, TALK AND LISTEN

1. Why is it difficult for some people to talk during or after sex about what is or isn't satisfying?
2. What part of sex and lovemaking makes you feel nervous or insecure?

Negotiate Frequency

The most common point of division seems to be frequency. One partner wants sex often. The other wants the experience only now and then.

On the one hand, even the Bible encourages couples not to withhold from one another, unless it's for a season of prayer—a kind of sexual fasting.[37] It goes on to say that by withholding, temptations become more powerful. Like it or not, this is absolutely true and sound advice. If you withhold sex from your

---

37 1 Corinthians 7:5.

partner you are withholding intimacy and creating more room for weakness and opportunity to collide. Even the strongest and most devoted people have moments of weakness. Keep them as few and far between as possible.

On the other hand, we're not animals. Self-control is a mark of personal maturity and a fruit of the Holy Spirit. If I "have to have it," even against the wishes of my spouse, then I've got some serious growing up to do.

Again, give and take. Be kind and generous, not controlling or manipulative. Talk honestly about hopes and preferences and build together an approach to meeting each others' needs. Even the nicest couples can experience tension when wants or needs go uncommunicated. So find the right words and ways to serve each other well.

"But when she doesn't want me, I feel unwanted … hurt … even angry. She gave me every reason to believe that we'd be hot and heavy in our sexual intimacy. It feels cool and light. She gave me the bait-and-switch!"

Maybe. More likely, something has changed. For some people, part of the mystique of sex wanes through the years. For others, unresolved issues from past experiences—even abusive ones—hamper an enthusiastic approach to sex. For still others, fatigue sets in when life gets hard. Or unresolved conflict makes sexual interactions feel inauthentic and forced.

Again, talk. Clear the air. Understand, accept and forgive each other. Get a counselor to help, if need be. Don't let this beautiful part of marriage become a huge sore spot.

STOP, TALK AND LISTEN

1. If you're already wary about frequency issues, start talking. What are your hopes and fears?
2. Can you imagine or predict emotional issues that will affect your approach to sexuality?

affection

How Much Is Too Much?

Another sore spot can be style and experimentation. One partner might like things spicy and creative, while the other prefers more "ordinary" approaches.

This is tough. No one should be forced beyond their comfort levels. But neither should one partner thwart the appetites and enthusiasms of the other (as long as they are safe and not harmful). Negotiate. Help each other. Accept each other.

STOP, TALK AND LISTEN

1. Do you have a similar craving for sexual adventure, or are there differences in hopes and willingness to try experimentation?

And Remember the Seasons

Men, women's lives and bodies cycle in ways that we'll never understand. The menstrual cycle creates moods and allergies to sex that should not be taken personally. Premenstrual Syndrome (PMS) is *not* a joke! It's real. Don't tease about it and don't try to wish it away. Not all women, but many women, suffer during those few days before a period. So think of those days as an opportunity to love her and serve her in other ways. Be supportive and be an active listener. We can't fix this.

Pregnancy can affect sexuality. Though most pregnancies are not impacted by sex, it's still time for men to be doubly sensitive and supportive. Some women report a growing sexual interest during pregnancy. Others report a lessened interest. Either way, now is the time to pour on the right kind of affection. Keep reminding her that there's nothing more beautiful than a woman carrying your child. And if we're lamenting the loss of her bikini figure, we need to grow up. It should bother us that some men have affairs and leave their wives during a time when joy should be at an all-time high.

By the way, ladies, a man's sex drive will likely not go away during pregnancy. You can help with this, whenever and however. I know that it's easy to pour your energy into the new life growing inside, but please save some energy and care for your husband.

After the birth of a child, sexual intercourse is on hold for many weeks. Again, guys, this is not the time to pressure her. And ladies, it's not the time to be so lost in your baby that you have no affection left for your husband. Some men actually experience depression and real anger when their wives no longer have relational energy for anyone but the baby. And some women feel exhausted and relationally depleted. Talk. Help each other through this wonderful and bleary-eyed season.

Body change can also affect sexual experience. Women say that body image—whether they feel good about their bodies—affects sexual enjoyment and performance. For the woman, it seems smart to do enough exercise and self-care so that you can feel good about your body. No, you'll likely never be a model or movie star. So what! Don't let life and body changes steal your sense of personal beauty and don't set yourself up with ridiculous and unhealthy expectations. You *are* beautiful! Men, tell her she's beautiful and accept her the way she is. If change is affecting sexual intimacy, find the right time and manner to talk about it.

Menopause can bring life changes to women that alter the sexual landscape. Some women feel free from the yucks of the menstrual cycle and report increased interest in sex. Other women feel a loss of drive with the change in hormonal activity. Talk. Men, be helpful. Women, be generous and transparent. If he doesn't know what you're experiencing, he'll be clumsy in his efforts to come alongside.

For men, depression, loss of a job, feelings of personal failure, retirement and any kind of stress can affect sexual interest and performance. Women, be sensitive and nonjudgmental. Pressure will not help him perform. Pile on the affection without as much interest in outcomes. It's likely just a season. Men *hate* being embarrassed, by the way. So don't tease about this. It's not funny and it won't help.

It might surprise you, ladies, that some men use sex as anesthetic. While problems at home or work might make you *less likely* to want sex, men will often use sex as escapism. In other words, you have the privilege of helping him reduce stress and take his mind off of problems elsewhere. This is a generous tool for love and support.

It seems like God has a dark sense of humor when we see that a man's midlife crisis often coincides with a woman's menopause. Gear up for that season and don't let it reach out and ruin all that you've built together. Surround yourselves with good friends. Practice healthy communication and generous sensitivity to each others' life changes. Endure.

STOP, TALK AND LISTEN

1. Talk about seasons and cycles. How have they already affected your affections?
2. Give each other reassurances and vows about "staying with you through life's seasons."

Different Wiring

As for the experience of sex, I'm glad that our pastor reminded us of this: men are like microwaves and women are like Crock-Pots. Men can usually fire up in an instant. For women, the best experiences are slow cooked.

Women say that they can be stimulated quite successfully by seeing a man helping around the house, and not by seeing him naked. Men, a timely gift or act of kindness can often prime the pump more than dirty talk or romantic theatrics.

Men are most stimulated by women who seem genuinely interested. And like it or not, appearance matters to most men. Not perfection, but care and attention to personal appearance.

The differences are fun and even funny. Please don't resent them. Resentment leads nowhere good. Accept these differences and maximize the upside.

And remember that for some couples the stereotypes are reversed. The man is the Crock-Pot and the woman is the microwave. No problem. Just learn and negotiate.

And don't judge your sex lives compared to anyone else. You're not married to anyone else. Accept this and go forward together.

Finally, find comfort in knowing that some couples have strong, intimate marriages even when sexuality has become almost impossible to express. Illness or injury that inhibits sexuality is not the end of a marriage. If, God forbid, you experience such things, figure it out and go forward. Many marvelous couples have simply reproportioned their intimacy in other ways. Again, other *building blocks* are more important.

STOP, TALK AND LISTEN

1. Talk about differences. Does the microwave or the Crock-Pot description fit you?
2. What would you do if sex became impossible?

No One Fell In and No One Falls Out

In this sex-crazed culture, some people build everything on sex and then run away when things lose their sizzle. Please, don't be like that. Our whole civilization comes apart at the seams when marriage suffers from this kind of "I fell out of love" immaturity. No one falls in and no one falls out of love. Your love was built on a succession of decisions and responses. It can fall apart in the same way.

So let sexuality bind you together and perform its magic. Grow to love *new* sex and *old* sex, the way that new things thrill and old things comfort and reinforce. You can do this, and you can even do it well.

"What Ifs" and "What Abouts"

What if my partner just won't flex? I want things a certain way, but I'm willing to flex on frequency and experimentation.

Some people simply have a hard time meeting half way and negotiating middle ground. Keep communicating your hope without nagging, badgering or manipulating.

My story of past sexuality is pretty sordid. My partner's is squeaky clean. How do we deal with this?

Both you and your partner need to find a peace with *your* past and *his/her* past. If this becomes a sore spot, it can inhibit your best efforts. Try to deeply understand the life circumstances that fueled your previous experiences. Offer acceptance and grace wherever possible. Give only as much detail as necessary —complete honesty but not specific details. Your future hopes have to be truth based, so don't be too secretive about the past. But put the past in the past. Live forward!

I've watched my parents live a sexless, passionless, romanceless marriage. Yuck! How do I avoid this?

Keep communicating about everything. Resolve issues or else they will stack up. Talk about sexual matters when you can muster the nerve, and don't ever give up.

But I know people who have given up. They've stopped giving themselves sexually.

How tragic and mean. Of course, there might be marriages with such deep and heinous wrongs suffered that sex seems impossible. But in most cases I'm aware of, one partner has simply become cold, stubborn, unforgiving and mean about withholding. Or else depression has reshaped the entire personality of the holdout.

What if I am sexually attached or addicted to my fiancé, and there aren't many other shared building blocks?

Simple answer: break off the engagement. Or at least put physical affection on hold long enough to evaluate whether the relationship has anything strong to build on.

My partner thinks that all affection and touching is foreplay. Hasn't anyone told him that women enjoy back rubs, foot rubs, hand-holding and a warm embrace—sometimes even more than sex? Do all things have to lead to sex?

No. Men, pay attention to this question. Sometimes, affection doesn't have to lead to sex. Let it be an end in itself.

Now, ladies, pay attention. Affection and touch will fire up his machinery in ways that are often difficult to shut down. Be sympathetic, not resentful. He's built to fire up. Be flattered by his interest, not frustrated by his hormones.

CHAPTER 18

more tools
to build with

In any field or pursuit,
people who are willing to work hard
and learn the skills
will flourish.

W hile it's hard to assign the pieces of this chapter to any one core value, these principles and behaviors are critically important to the quality of a marriage. I offer these insights as a kind of dessert after the main course. Some reiterate or expand coaching from previous chapters.

About Conflict Resolution

Whatever other authors say, I believe that suffering marriages are usually the result of unresolved conflict or dysfunctional conflict resolution styles. Figure out what works for you in order to resolve inevitable conflict. If you are someone who needs space to process your feelings, tell your partner, "I need space to process my feelings." Then, so he or she needn't worry that you won't come back, say, "I'll be back soon." I call that giving a *cue*—a brief sentence that helps your partner know what you feel or need.

If you're someone who chases the other person in order to resolve as quickly as possible, make sure that's what your

more tools to build with

partner needs or wants. If not, learn to wait until you're both ready to talk. Forcing resolution is like pushing a rope. It's an insecure feeling to wait, but you can.

If you're a door slammer and a spoon thrower, fine—as long as you don't hurt anyone. But be prepared that your partner might find those theatrics to be a huge put-off. That kind of outburst will probably delay resolution and will likely need to be modified.

If you're someone who clams up when you're angry, realize that ultimately you need to communicate. If your silence is punishment, get over it as quickly as possible. You are not your partner's parent, or judge and jury of the household. Punishment is not your job. If your silence comes from restraint ("I don't want to say anything that I'll regret later,") then *bravo*. Keep holding on until your feelings can be spoken in a less hurtful, nonaccusative tone. Use words like, "When this happens, this is how I feel," rather than, "You make me so mad when you...."

If your silence is a passive way of getting attention, it will likely be ineffective. Your partner is not a mind reader and will eventually get frustrated by the ridiculous burden of interpreting and responding to childish silence. As parents often tell their children, "Use your words."

Again, figure out what works for you two. If screaming and arguing works, fine, as long as it leads to resolution. If it helps for one person to leave for a while, okay, as long as the space allows for processing and resolution. If the two of you have divergent approaches to conflict, find the intersection where your approaches connect and learn how to build dialogue and understanding at that intersection.

Remember, the need to be right will delay conflict resolution forever. Let it go! Understand, accept and respect. Those are the steps that lead to resolution.

Also:

- Apologize every time.
- Forgive every time.

- Do not let resentments build up over many days.
- Stop the name-calling.
- If there's a backup of unresolved conflicts, call a counselor to help you sift and sort.
- If you fight in front of the kids, make sure they see the resolution or hear you describe how you resolved the issue. Kids need to learn good conflict resolution skills by watching you, and the perception of unresolved conflict is disconcerting for kids. And, don't fight badly in front of the kids. It frightens them.
- Choose a good setting for the hard talks—like your favorite coffee shop. You have to behave in public and the setting might relax you some.
- Own your own anger level. You are responsible for staying in the realm of fair fighting. The other person might have hurt or disappointed you, but you are responsible for maintaining the level of your temper.
- And, yes, some of us have an innate ability to push buttons and give zingers that set off the anger in the other—and then claim the high ground because we're "not the angry one!" Again, each person is responsible for his/her own anger levels, but still—we can be very nasty about how we push buttons and escalate conflict. Either start being more helpful or you'll keep suffering escalations.
- Finally, listen, listen, listen to each other.

STOP, TALK AND LISTEN

1. What do you typically do with your anger? How do you behave?
2. What brings the two of you back together? What works? What doesn't work?
3. Are there buttons to absolutely avoid in the midst of conflict? Why?

more tools to build with

About Bossiness

Don't be bossy, *ever,* for any reason. You are not the boss. Bossy behavior is a brutal corrosive in any marriage. No one likes to be bossed around by a spouse—no one, not ever. And no bossy spouses will feel good about being bossy for very long. If your partner is bossy and has a blind spot about it, now would be a good time to say, "It seems important for me to tell you that bossiness makes me feel belittled; like less than an equal partner. I've had parents growing up, and I have a boss at work. In our home, I'm not sure I'm supposed to have a boss, am I?"

Men, women don't want to mother us. But sometimes, we put them into that position by our inattention to household needs. We need to show up, pay attention and be part of the solution to everyday problems in the home.

Please, ladies—men *hate* to be mothered. Some women develop this bad habit for all kinds of reasons. Break the habit! It will push him away. Be smart and stop. As my kids would say to each other, "You're not the boss of me."

Over the years, it's become more rare to see husbands being bossy in American culture. When it happens, we see dominant, high-control men man-handling exhausted wives. In some cases, older men marry younger women because the additional years give relational leverage for greater control. But as years go by, she often grows stronger and more self-assured, no longer ready to be shackled by a male-dominant model. The whole household goes through a metamorphosis—for better or worse, depending on how he receives the changes in the system. Sadly, he might have married a younger woman because of his insecurities and the need to be in charge. Younger women, be careful. It might feel good today to be marrying a man who will take care of you. But the day might be coming soon when you feel like you're smothered under the blanket of his "care." Make sure that you are an equal partner right from the start.

STOP, TALK AND LISTEN

1. Who called the shots growing up—your mom or your
   dad? Was there visible give and take? Compromise? Distribution of tasks?
2. How do you feel about the distribution of tasks and
   authority in your relationship? Do you feel heard? Respected? Controlled? Bossed? Talk!

About Households of Origin

The families that you've come from play an ever-important
part in your marriage. You must talk about your parents and
the household systems that will inform your approach to home
and family.

First, find out the parents' approach to relationship. If your
partner's parents had a cold but functional relationship, your
partner might be predisposed that way. Unless cold but functional is what you're looking for, you'd better probe to make
sure that your partner is absolutely committed to something
warmer. If not, you will see your partner do what he was taught
to do or follow the patterns she watched in her parents.

Second, if your partner's parents divorced, beware and ask
a host of hard questions. "How do I know you won't pull out
when things get tough?" Honestly, children of divorce are usually very determined not to divorce—but since they've survived
one divorce, they know subconsciously that they could survive
another. For those of us whose parents endured and stayed
married, divorce can be unimaginable. Children of divorce are
simply more likely to divorce. So there are hard questions to
ask and resolve.

Third, who wore the pants? Sometimes one partner comes
from a matriarchal or patriarchal home, and then expects the
other to participate gladly in a one-party-dominant system.

more tools to build with

Even when the first partner is willing to be *dominated* instead of *dominator,* this subtle expectation can place a huge load on the other. When I ask couples to describe their parents' decision-making practices, most of them say, "Mom pretty much called the shots. Dad was either absent or a kind of figurehead in the home." Most young couples today seem adamant about finding shared approaches that defy caricatures of dominant-mom and placated-dad models.

Fourth, be absolutely sure about patterns of abuse and addiction in every family. If there has been physical, sexual, drug, alcohol or verbal abuse in either family of origin, make sure that considerable steps have been taken to pursue healing and to break the chain of abuse. If not, those deeply embedded problems are likely to resurface in your generation. That would be catastrophic for your high hopes. Work together on this. Now is not the time to be naïve about the terrible effects of abuse and addiction, or to think, "That could never happen to me." Get the help you need for these tough matters.

Finally, talk at length about the quirks of your families. Did we fight at the Thanksgiving table or were we happy? What are the expectations for family visits—once a year, once a month or once a week? How often will we be talking to our mothers? How much meddling or real help should we expect in child-rearing? Are the apron strings properly snipped, or is there going to be an issue with confused loyalties?

By the way, you belong to your partner now. Don't be confused. He or she is now your first loyalty under God. Even after kids are born, the best way you can love your kids is to love your spouse and be models of healthy relationship-building. Children need less coddling and more modeling.

STOP, TALK AND LISTEN

1. Describe your parents' relationships. Pros and cons; episodes and observations.
2. What have you learned from them in the positive sense—things you hope to mimic?
3. What have you learned in the negative sense—things you hope to leave behind? How do you intend to do this?
4. What about outright quirks and weirdness? Anything you should warn your partner about in your family?

Money Matters

Couples tend to fight about money. Here are a few reminders and suggestions.

First, come to an agreement on your hopes. If one person values a mansion in the hills and the other person dreams of a cottage in a cozy neighborhood, you have some negotiating to do. If one wants an extravagant life and the other a simple one, there might be fundamental differences in core values. Be careful and talk this through. This issue will affect numerous other issues, like how many hours to work, whether to pursue promotion, whether to relocate often, and whether to spend or save.

Second, establish a budget and stick to it. It sounds simple; it isn't. But it's important. Make it realistic and workable. Often a frugal person hooks up with a free-spending person because the two offset and help each other. So make sure that the frugal partner doesn't have to constantly badger the big spender, or else conflict will grow and grow. In my family, my wife is frugal. I value the way she helps me check careless, spontaneous impulses to spend, and I help her cut loose every now and then. It's a good balance as long as we're honest with our feelings and united in our broader hopes.

more tools to build with

Third, distribute tasks and responsibilities carefully. Again, my wife handles the checkbook better than me, so it's hers. And I can wade through mortgage documents better than her, so they're mine.

Fourth, be honest. Don't harbor any silly secrets or play relational games with money. Too much resentment can build up if trust is broken in this area.

Fifth, arrive at specific amounts that can be spent without having to call the other for the go-ahead. I can usually play a round of golf without asking (a hundred bucks) but I can't buy a new car independently. It's not *my* money. It's *our* money. I have a partner in this enterprise called life. "But I earned it; I can spend it," say some painfully self-absorbed people. No. You belong to each other and the money you earn belongs to the family. Do it together, unless you agree on specific exceptions.

Finally, give to God, give to others and establish a culture of generosity in the home. Whether you believe in Jesus or Karma or some other code of reality, "Whoever sows sparingly will also reap sparingly, and whoever sows generously will also reap generously."[38] Those words from the Bible teach a critical life value—generous people are happier in every way. Enjoy giving together creatively and consistently. Teach this way of life to your children. Be a contributor in your church and community.

STOP, TALK AND LISTEN

1. Which one of you is the saver and which is the spender?
2. Describe your ultimate home and living environments. Negotiate differences and seek clear understanding.
3. How hard are you willing to work and how much do you want to sacrifice to make money? Make sure you're on the same page.
4. Talk about roles. Who has the checkbook? Who handles investments, insurance and mortgage matters?

---

38 2 Corinthians 9:6.

Hope versus Expectation

One marriage-killer is expectation. It's like bossiness—a corrosive. Any tone of expectation creates a superiority-versus-inferiority platform. You're not the boss and you really can't expect anything. If you do, your partner will either shrivel or simmer under the influence of expectations—and likely rebel.

Hope, on the other hand, is not as disappointing. Communicate every hope in a freehanded way and watch how your partner is eager to see your hopes and dreams come true.

Do you really want a dutiful and obedient slave, or do you want a life partner? Partners in love have hopes. High hopes, of course, but hopes.

I know that we communicate our vows in the language of covenant loyalty, and it seems right to expect our spouse to be true to those vows. But even then, a *kept* person is more likely to strain against the chains. Someone who is loved freely and treated with dignity is more likely to stay without any chains.

Freedom makes every relationship authentic. Expectation ties burdens around the other. Hope is free and unfettered, and it fuels our best instincts for loyalty and love.

"But I've been hurt before! I'm afraid. I expect my new husband to treat me right." Of course. Communicate that pain as an expectation and he will love you as if you are a wounded victim. I suggest that you pursue every kind of healing and then take the risk of loving again in a hopeful, freehanded way. Communicate your vulnerability honestly. He'll respect you and be far more likely not to hurt you in the realm of your vulnerability.

All this to say, controlling people often do badly in marriage. Though controllers tend to marry exceptionally cooperative people, the spouse usually grows weary of overbearing treatment. If you are a controller by nature, get help, get humble and appeal to your partner for understanding while you learn the art of hope vs. expectation.

more tools to build with

STOP, TALK AND LISTEN

1. Make two lists of things each of you hope for in marriage. Now read them aloud to each other, not as expectations but as hopes.
2. Do you ever feel crushed by the weight of the other person's expectations? Describe.

Give Me a Cue

Communicating hope means offering your partner a cue to your happiness. The practice of giving cues came to me after fifteen years of marriage. When the value of giving cues presented itself, my own marriage and other marriages have benefitted greatly.

Here's an example: I'm on my way home from work, exhausted. I walk in the door to see that my wife has been alone with small children all day. She's tired, too. In the past, we might have slogged through, assuming each others' feelings and needs. Now, I'm in the habit of offering a cue or asking for one. In some cases, I might say, "Sue, I need fifteen minutes to change my clothes and decompress. Then I'll take the kids." In other cases, I'll ask, "Tell me what you need tonight," so she can give me a cue.

In worst-case scenarios, I might say, "I'm tired and grouchy. I'm trying to be civil and social; but if I can have one hour to be a vegetable, I promise you that I'll be a lot more fun tonight."

In other words, don't leave things unsaid. Don't assume or expect the other to assume hopes or feelings. "Tell me what you need" is a generous proposal. "Can I tell you what I need?" is a smart question.

No one can read minds!

"Today, I feel a need for space. Don't be offended. It's just how I feel." That works so much better than put-offish behavior and moodiness that's loaded with insinuations that say, "Get away from me!"

Even in conflict, a cue can be a lifesaver. "I'm feeling angry. Are you ready to hear me, or should I wait for a better time?" The other partner can say, "I care about how you feel, but I'm a bit fragile right now. Can you give me an hour?"

You might say, "Are you kidding? Who talks like that?" Well, people who want to lubricate relationship in ways that prevent corrosion and collision talk like that.

STOP, TALK AND LISTEN

1. Can you remember a time when a cue saved you from conflict or smoothed some tension?
2. Are either of you mind readers? Do either of you expect the other person to be one? Talk!

So Here We Go

Love each other extravagantly. Become masters at the other person's love language. Be mindful about how you can improve your partner's life every day. Give. Negotiate. Compromise. Communicate. Sacrifice. Play. Laugh. Get it on! Be gracious. Forgive. Do marriage on purpose. Learn the skills and behaviors that grow relationship.

Build carefully on a solid foundation. Your marriage will be unshakeable!

about the author

Keith Potter is a pastor, speaker, author and the Executive Director of Potter's Clay, a non-profit that inspires and equips marriages (**www.UnshakableMarriage.com**), leaders (**www.ChampionProject.com**) and churches (**www.Abraham Projectonline.org**).

As a marriage coach, Keith has presented *Unshakable Marriage Workshops* around the United States and in Europe. He is the host and founder of the *Marriage Café* movement (**www.MarriageCafeOnline.com**) and teaches *Don't Lose Before You Choose conferences* to singles and students at universities and high schools. Keith addresses *Marriage and the Masculine Soul* at men's conferences and his long career in ministry prompts Keith to give special care to *Marriage and the Pastor's Soul.*

A Pacific Northwest native, Keith holds bachelors, masters and doctoral degrees from Northwest Christian University and Fuller Seminary, and studied at Western Washington University, the University of Oregon and Bethel Seminary.

Keith and Sue Potter have three children, Kristen (married to Joe Cabalka), Erin and Luke. They live in Temecula, California, where Keith enjoys writing and reading fiction, playing and watching sports and being a husband and dad.

acknowledgments

As the Second Edition of *Unshakable* finds it's voice, I'm grateful for the partnership of so many people who've contributed to the content and distribution of these thoughts.

First, I think of the hundreds of couples that I've married since 1984. Our deep and important conversations in preparation for marriage have fueled this project. Our "building blocks" exercise is the blueprint for the whole book. So each couple should be able to find a fingerprint somewhere on these pages.

Then I think of the married couples that grant me a window into their best practices, profound pain and earnest hopes for a healthy marriage. For all the great models of sturdy, stubborn commitment and love, I'm grateful; and for those who are scraping to get there, you have my hope and respect.

This book borrows from the thoughts of many others—authors, counselors, pastors and teachers. I'm grateful for all the schools I've been able to swim in, and continue to hope that this tool is useful for your important work in helping others.

Brenna Hall is a smart, talented Executive Assistant. Add the expertise of Tim Beals and Credo Communications, and the Second Edition is a snap. The Board and Friends of Potter's Clay (www.pottersclayonline.org) make the Unshakable Marriage Project (www.unshakablemarriage.com) possible. Partners like Ronnie and Karen Lott are invaluable.

Family continues to inspire my work. It makes a world of difference that my wife, Sue, continues to learn and grow beside me as a fellow student of marriage and life. I'm awed by her ability to love me *well* and *a lot*. Since the First Edition, our daughter Kristen has married Joe Cabalka, and their fresh commitment and hearty approach to building their relationship encourages me. At home, Erin and Luke keep Sue and me laughing, which only infuses happiness into marriage.

Once again, I honor Paul and Virginia Wright (Sue's parents) and Glen and Verian Potter (my parents) for their loyalty to the covenant of marriage. By staying together, they've modeled and implanted irreplaceable faith in the value of making it work through the seasons of life.